CARMEL, MONTEREY
& PACIFIC GROVE

Getaway Guide to California's Monterey Peninsula

DAVID VOKAC & JOAN VOKAC

Vokac, David, 1940–
    Carmel, Monterey & Pacific Grove:
        Getaway Guide to California's
        Monterey Peninsula
David Vokac & Joan Vokac. — 1st ed.
    p. cm.
    Includes index.
    ISBN-13: 978-0-930743-33-8

    1. Monterey, California—Guidebooks. 2. Cities and
towns—Monterey, California—Guidebooks. 3. Monterey,
California—History, Local. 4. Carmel, California—Guidebooks.
5. Cities and towns—Carmel, California—Guidebooks.
6. Carmel, California—History, Local. 7. Pacific Grove,
California—Guidebooks. 8. Cities and towns—Pacific Grove,
California—Guidebooks. 9. Pacific Grove, California—History,
Local. I. Vokac, Joan, 1948– II. Title.

First Edition
1 2 3 4 5 6 7 8 9 10
Manufactured in the United States of America

PREFACE

The only place in the country where three of the 100 **Great Towns of America** adjoin is on the Monterey Peninsula. No surprise, given the combination of a spectacular coastline; a climate as ideal for human habitation as it is for lush landscapes; and natural constraints that slowed urban land development long enough for political sentiments to take over the role of protecting this unique natural setting from rampant growth.

Three distinct towns grew side-by-side from very different sources. Monterey was the first to boom. In fact, it was the first permanent settlement in California, and the first of Spain's four presidios. Its calm ocean on the leeward side of Monterey Bay made it an ideal seaport for a thriving fishing industry. Carmel followed closely behind with the establishment of a mission in a captivating setting where artistic souls later found their muse. Pacific Grove was the last to be founded—as a summer retreat for Methodists, where serenity and orderliness reigned for nearly a century. Each town's roots are still delightfully reflected in their evolving personalities, even though now all of them share the challenges of their enormous appeal to travelers from all over the world.

With incomparable beauty, there is plenty for visitors to enjoy year-round. A hike/bike path connects Monterey and Pacific Grove with flowery seascapes to within a block of famed historic Cannery Row; and the Seventeen Mile Drive is one of America's most picturesque scenic roads. Everyone should take time to stroll among storybook cottages in downtown Carmel, and marvel at how roads always yield rights of way to noble trees. Kayaking, hiking, fishing, boating and other sports are delightful in world-class land-and-sea settings from the Peninsula through Big Sur bounding the region on the south. The Monterey Aquarium is one of the finest in the nation. Lush landscapes and romantic settings have spawned sybaritic spas and romantic retreats in all three towns. Wineries and affiliated tasting rooms abound, as does gourmet food in all styles and price levels. Weather is hospitable most of the year. The only problems facing travelers is that there are so many of them. Traffic jams are always possible, restaurant queues can be long, and lodging prices (particularly on weekends) can be daunting. Happily, the livability rewards are more than worth it. This guidebook will help you discover the marvels of this remarkable area.

CONTENTS

Carmel, California

HISTORY & DESCRIPTION

Carmel is one of the world's loveliest collaborations between land and sea. On the southern side of the Monterey Peninsula, the unique seaside village sequestered in a forest of rare Monterey cypress borders a slope of fine white sand that extends into the surf of Carmel Bay. The idyllic site remained undeveloped until 1771, when Father Junipero Serra built a mission near where the area's major stream, the Carmel River, empties into Carmel Bay and the Pacific Ocean. He built here a year after the first permanent settlement in California was established at the Presidio in Monterey in 1770 to take advantage of the area's main source of year-round fresh water and better land for growing crops.

It wasn't until more than a century later that artists and writers began building houses in the pines. They were attracted by the captivating location and potential for a simple lifestyle. The sensitivity of these artists and dreamers fostered the charm that is still being nurtured. Fairy tale cottages and fanciful houses and shops are a highly visible part of the legacy. Another part is the residents' continuing determination to retain the beauty and serenity of this place in spite of its overwhelming popularity. As a result, the village still does not have: traffic lights, parking meters, neon signs, billboards, street lights outside the business district, buildings more than three stories high, or home mail delivery. Today, it does have a compact downtown with an astonishing proliferation of notable places to stroll, shop, eat, drink, and sleep.

More than eighty distinctive galleries display everything from local to international quality arts and crafts. In addition, all sorts of non-chain specialty shops compete for the stroller's attention. So do bonanzas of gourmet dining and drinking venues and architecturally unique lodgings, most of which cater to romance.

WEATHER

Bordering the Pacific Ocean on the southern curve of the Monterey Peninsula, Carmel has one of America's most desirable climates. Pleasant weather for most outdoor activities is the rule except during winter. Then, days and evenings are cool, but seldom include a frost or snow of any consequence. Occasional heavy rainstorms during this season contribute well over half of the average annual precipitation. Spring marks the beginning of many months of mild weather for enjoying outdoor activities in light sportswear. The appeal of warm days, cool evenings, and diminishing showers is offset somewhat by sea breezes and coastal fog common during this season. Summer weather is excellent. In addition to uniformly warm days and cool nights, there is no rainfall. But, late night and early morning fog along the coast is recurrent in this naturally air-conditioned seaside playground at this most popular time of year. Fall is a surprising improvement of summer, with less fog and daytime temperatures early in the season that are normally the year's highest. Splendid conditions continue until around Thanksgiving when the rainy season begins again in earnest.

WEATHER PROFILE

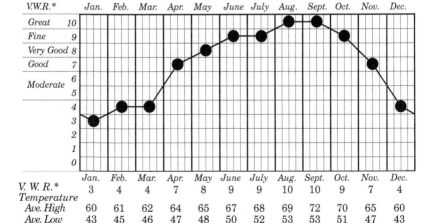

V.W.R.*	Jan.	Feb.	Mar.	Apr.	May	June	July	Aug.	Sept.	Oct.	Nov.	Dec.
V. W. R.*	3	4	4	7	8	9	9	10	10	9	7	4
Temperature												
Ave. High	60	61	62	64	65	67	68	69	72	70	65	60
Ave. Low	43	45	46	47	48	50	52	53	53	51	47	43
Precipitation												
Inches Rain	4.2	3.2	3.5	1.5	0.5	0.2	0.1	0.1	0.3	1.1	2.1	3.0
Inches Snow	-	-	-	-	-	-	-	-	-	-	-	-

V. W. R. = Vokac Weather Rating; probability of mild (warm and dry) weather on any given day.

ATTRACTIONS

★ **Bicycling**
One of America's finest auto/bicycle rides (the Seventeen-Mile Drive) and other scenic routes provide access to the coastline, mountains and bucolic valleys around Carmel. Rental bicycles by the hour or longer are available from:
Adventures by the Sea *(831)648-7235*
adventuresbythesea.com
(see listing in Monterey)
Bay Bikes *(831)624-7433*
1 mi. SE at 3600 The Barnyard
baybikes.com
Big Sur Coast *(831)667-2315*
S for approximately 80 mi. on Highway 1
bigsurcalifornia.org
California Highway 1 was completed in 1937. Today it is one of the world's most exhilarating scenic drives. A narrow, paved two-lane road winds and dips along the flanks of a mountain wilderness rising precipitously from an unspoiled Pacific Ocean shoreline. Numerous hiking trails lead into groves of the southernmost coast redwoods on the continent in sheltered fern-shaded canyons, and to remote sandy beaches and coves. Well-located state parks along the route offer memorable camping and picnicking opportunities. Unique galleries, restaurants and lodgings blend harmoniously into the countryside, each artistically reflecting the unique charm of the Big Sur, adding to the pleasure of this memorable drive. *As a convenience to readers, all Big Sur features are listed together in the section below by highway driving distance from downtown Carmel.*
Rocky Point Restaurant *(831)624-2933*
13 mi. S at 36700 Highway 1 - Big Sur
rockypointrestaurant.com
L–D.   *Expensive*
Contemporary California cuisine, featuring entrees like fisherman's cioppino or slow-roasted prime rib, have to compete with a floor-to-ceiling window-wall view of Pacific Ocean headlands just below. Several dining areas and popular expansive dining terraces maximize the seaside setting.

★ **Bixby Bridge**
  15 mi. S on Highway 1 - Big Sur
  This is the most spectacular of many bridges completed during the Great Depression to transform a coastal wilderness into a remarkable drive. Turnouts are available near either end so that travelers can marvel at this classic of harmonized manmade and natural grandeur.

★ **Molera Big Sur Horseback Riding**   *(831)625-5486*
  23 mi. S in Andrew Molera State Park - Big Sur
  molerahorsebacktours.com
  Scenic horse riding tours can be reserved for from 1 to 2.5 hours from a stable in the Andrew Molera State Park. Horseback riding by the surf and (on longer rides) among redwood trees is a truly memorable experience.

  Big Sur River Inn   *(831)667-2700*
  26 mi. S at 46840 Hwy. 1 at Pheneger Creek - Big Sur
  bigsurriverinn.com
  B–L–D.   *Expensive*
  Banana or berry pancakes, omelets, or pan-fried trout are breakfast highlights in a historic wood-trim dining room with a river-rock fireplace, a window-wall view of Big Sur River, plus dining terraces with forest and stream views. For a real treat, you can put your chair in the stream. A small motel and gift shop adjoin.

★ **Glen Oaks Big Sur**   *(831)667-2105*
  27 mi. S at 47080 Highway 1 - Big Sur
  glenoaksbigsur.com
  25 units   *Very Expensive*
  A cabin colony amidst lush grandeur featuring native redwoods has been thoroughly remodeled and upgraded for a 21st century country look. Each beautifully decorated unit has a raised gas fireplace, refrigerator and microwave, and a small private deck. Food is available at the **Big Sur Roadhouse** and nearby cafe/grocery.

★ **Pfeiffer-Big Sur State Park**   *(831)667-2315*
  29 mi. S at 47225 Highway 1 - Big Sur
  www.parks.ca.gov/?page_id=570
  Some of America's southernmost coast redwoods are a key feature of this popular park. Full-service campsites are

available for vehicles, bikes and hikers and lodging (see listing); dining, gift shop and grocery store are conveniently clustered among the redwoods. Many hiking and bike trails access surrounding mountains, forests and beaches.

★ **Big Sur Lodge**   *(831)667-3100   (800)424-4787*
   29 mi. S at 47225 Highway 1 - Big Sur 93920
   bigsurlodge.com
   B–L–D.   *Expensive*
   62 units   *Expensive–Very Expensive*
After the fashion of National Park lodges, Big Sur Lodge (located in the Pfeiffer Big Sur State Park) has a large fully-wood-trimmed dining room with floor-to-ceiling windows on three sides offering intimate views of surrounding redwood forests. Contemporary American fare is featured at all meals, and there is also a (weather permitting) large sunny deck by the big trees. Recently remodeled cabins and lodge rooms surrounded by a luxuriant redwood forest are near trailheads which lead into surrounding forested highlands and down the Big Sur River to the coast. Each hillside cottage-style room is comfortably furnished without distractions, but with a private deck. Several have a wood-burning fireplace and kitchen. A well-stocked gift shop and grocery store are in the Lodge.

★ **Big Sur Bakery & Restaurant**   *(831)667-0520*
   29 mi. S at 47540 Highway 1 - Big Sur
   bigsurbakery.com
   B–L–D. No D Mon.   *Expensive*
The Big Sur Bakery is Big Sur's quintessential source of traditional and creative pastries and light fare on an evolving ever-changing menu. The maple-bacon bow tie is a delightfully sophisticated blend of sweet and savory. For dessert, the blueberry-pecan upside-down cake with lemon cream and vanilla ice cream is memorable. Anything on the limited-but-thoughtful menu can be special. The classic Big Sur-style dining cottage has a display of the day's variety of pastries. Nearby are tables in a little wood-trim dining room, and outside in the shade of a giant redwood overlooking a remarkably large Australian protea bush (which blooms in April).

★ **Post Ranch Inn** *(831)667-2200 (800)527-2200*
30 mi. S at 47900 Highway 1 - Big Sur 93920
postranchinn.com
L–D.   *Very Expensive*
43 units   *Very Expensive*

Sierra Mar Restaurant at Post Ranch is one of America's most enchanting restaurants. This architectural jewel of wood, stone and glass crowns a rugged bluff more than a thousand feet above the heart of the Big Sur Coast. You feel like you are directly over the Pacific Ocean behind awe-inspiring floor-to-ceiling window walls. Advance reservations are required to partake of the four- or nine-course gourmet dinner or three-course lunch where artistically presented foods complement the astounding view. Every day the menu changes to reflect the freshest seasonal ingredients and the chef's whims. You make a selection from among about four options for each of the courses. Inspired creations prepared from top-quality seasonal ingredients result in individualized cutting-edge California cuisine. Caviar, foie gras, truffles and other epicurean ingredients are used for exciting presentations of dishes like curried mussel bisque, or roast venison loin with chestnut purée. Housemade desserts are similarly delicious. The delightful contemporary dining room is up a lengthy staircase on a forested hillside, which builds anticipation for the feast at the top. Full-length floor-to-ceiling windows maximize the spellbinding view from elegant tables adjacent to window alcoves along the blufftop. There is also a small bar which does not require a reservation, open to the general public as long as space allows.

Post Ranch Inn is the quintessential Big Sur luxury retreat. The grandeur of the site high above a rugged coast is perfectly matched by tranquil post-modern architecture and artistic decor seamlessly blended into luxuriant natural surroundings. Bountiful gourmet breakfast buffet including many items from their own garden is complimentary. Amenities include two whirlpools (both are "infinity" pools that provide a rimless overlook to a breathtaking coastline); exercise room; hiking trails to memorable locales; full-service spa treatments that only serve resort guests (like outdoor massage while on a table with an eagle's-eye view of the coastline far below); a large outdoor pool; a quality mercantile shop; and **Sierra Mar Restaurant**. Each uniquely decorated one-bedroom suite is luxuriously furnished, including a private view deck, wood-burning fireplace and large soaking bath. A small refrigerator with snacks and beverages, and champagne and wine on arrival, are complimentary.

"Ocean" (5 of these)—single structure; two-sided fireplace; ocean views from whirlpool, window seat, terrace.

"Coast" (10 of these)—circular duplex with ocean view from the whirlpool, terrace, or king bed.

★ **Ventana Inn & Spa**   *(831)667-2331   (800)628-6500*
30 mi. S at 48123 Highway 1 - Big Sur 93920
ventanainn.com
B–L–D.   Very Expensive
59 units   Very Expensive

In **The Restaurant at Ventana**, California cuisine is emphasized on a selected list from quality ingredients of the season. At dinner, each course can be ordered apart from the chef's four-course menu. Popular choices include housemade rabbit fettuccine, prime rib, and crispy artichokes, plus decadent housemade desserts. The wood-toned post-modern multilevel dining room provides expansive window views of the distant ocean and/or mountains. An adjoining umbrella-shaded terrace is even closer to the inspiring seascape far below. A woodcrafted firelit lounge adjoins.

Ventana Inn & Spa is a progenitor of posh post-modern architecture and decor in California lodgings. The enchanting country inn blends seamlessly into mountain ridges and meadows high above the Big Sur coast. Amenities of the adults-only inn include paved walking paths and nature trails through woodlands to coastal overlooks; two extra-long pools (one pool, the tubs and sauna are clothing-optional); two serene Japanese-style hot baths open to moonlight; sauna; exercise room; full-service spa with all sorts of revitalizing body and beauty treatments and boutique; art gallery; and **The Restaurant**. Gourmet Continental breakfast and afternoon wine and appetizers are complimentary. Each room is a luxuriously furnished study in upscale post-modern rusticity. Many have a private deck (some with a distant ocean view), wood-burning fireplace, and two-person whirlpool tub and refrigerator.

★ **Nepenthe** *(831)667-2345*
31 mi. S at 48510 Highway 1 - Big Sur
nepenthebigsur.com
L–D.   *Expensive*
After well over half a century, traditional American fare including a few house specialties like ambrosia burger (a ground steak sandwich with secret sauce on a french roll) or deep-dish apple pie continue to supplement the reason for Nepenthe's fame. The eternal grandeur of the setting has been nicely retained with window walls on two sides and dining terraces beyond offering unforgettable panoramas of miles of the magnificent Big Sur Coast more than eight hundred feet below. At **Cafe Kevah** (B–L), American and Mexican comfort foods and fruit pies are served on an umbrella-shaded terrace overlooking mountains and the sea. The **Phoenix Gift Shop** is a long-established top source of quality arts, crafts, books and treats of the region.

★ **Julia Pfeiffer Burns State Park** *(831) 667-2315*
39 mi. S at Milepost 37 South Highway 1 - Big Sur
www.parks.ca.gov/?page_id=578
Here is the setting for one of California's most famous pictures: a waterfall drops off a cliff onto a smooth-sand beach bordering a clear Pacific Ocean lagoon sheltered by rocky pine-accented promontories. Environmentally sensitive overnight campsites, scenic picnic areas, hiking trails, and some exhibits are available.

★ **Carmel Beach**
just W at the foot of Ocean Av.
carmelcalifornia.com/carmel-beach.htm
A picturesque beach is backed by a pine-studded slope of fine, dazzlingly white sand. Cold water and undertow preclude serious swimming year-round, but it is a wonderful place for strolling and enjoying magnificent sunsets.

★ **Carmel Mission Basilica**   *(831)624-1271*
1 mi. S (off Hwy. 1) at 3080 Rio Rd. (at Lasuen Dr.)
carmelmission.org
The key link to early California history was established on this site overlooking the mouth of the Carmel River in 1771 by Father Junipero Serra ("Father of the California missions"). It was his residence and headquarters until his death in 1784. He is buried beneath the present sandstone church, which was completed in 1797. The carefully restored mission's museum has a notable collection of his memorabilia and historic relics.

★ **Carmel River State Beach**   *(831)649-2836*
1 mi. S on Scenic Rd.
parks.ca.gov
A photogenic ocean beach composed of fine white sand beckons beachcombers, sunbathers and picnickers. It is unsuitable for swimming any time because of cold water and currents.

★ **Downtown**
Carmel has one of America's most enchanting walking districts full of surprises. Thatched cottages and compatible contemporary structures plus lush vegetation, flowers and artworks distinguish a specialty shopping and dining bonanza.

Golf
Pebble Beach Resort's Courses
pebblebeach.com/golf
The Monterey Peninsula is sometimes described as "the greatest meeting of land and sea in the world." After more than a century, the public championship 18-hole golf courses described here are, collectively, America's most splendid contribution to the game of golf. Each is a landmark admired as much for its beauty as for links and greens showcasing breathtaking natural grandeur of pine-forested hills, dunes and the Pacific coast. All have complete facilities and refined restaurants and lodgings.

★   **Links at Spanish Bay**   *(831)574-5607*
6 mi. NW at 2700 Seventeen-Mile Dr. - Pebble Beach
pebblebeach.com/golf
This is a true rugged Scottish-style links that is also one of the most ecologically sensitive golf courses. Features include expansive views of Pacific beaches, meadows and dunes. Each day, at sunset, a bagpiper closes the course.

★ **Pebble Beach Golf Links** *(831)574-5609*
2 mi. NW at 1700 Seventeen-Mile Dr. - Pebble Beach
America's #1 public golf course (according to Golf Digest) is
renowned for its classic seaside greens and holes, remarkable
beauty, and century-long heritage as a host of championship
tournaments backed by a remarkable diversity of related
resort facilities.

★ **Spyglass Hill Golf Course** *(831)574-5608*
3 mi. NW at 3206 Stevenson Dr. - Pebble Beach
After more than half a century, one of the world's top golf
courses is still one of the toughest, with fairways ranging
from dense forests to sandy Pacific Coast shoreline. Complete
on-site facilities include a pro shop.

Rancho Canada Golf Course *(831)624-0111 (800)536-9459*
3 mi. SE at 4860 Carmel Valley Rd. - Carmel Valley
ranchocanada.com
Two well-regarded 18-hole golf courses offer fairways that
meander along picturesque Carmel River are popular because
of scenic and often-sunny Carmel Valley. Food service, putting
green and driving range are also available.

Horseback Riding
Another way to see the grandeur of the Monterey Peninsula
coast is via a horseback ride. Four times daily, near-beach trail
rides of 75 minutes take you down to a blufftop along the Pacific
Coast where you can enjoy watching the surf roll in while you
are aboard a quarterhorse (if one is available). Forest trail rides
are also available four times a day for 50-minute rides. Rides
and lessons can be reserved at the equestrian center.

Pebble Beach Equestrian Center *(866)923-8964*
3 mi. NW at 3300 Portola Rd. - Pebble Beach
pebblebeach.com

★ **Point Lobos State Reserve** *(831)624-4909*
5 mi. S at 62 Highway 1
parks.ca.gov
One of the most beautiful reserves on the Pacific coast includes
six miles of headlands, secluded coves, tidepools, sea lion
rocks, and a natural grove of rare Monterey cypress. The
setting inspired Robert Louis Stevenson's *Treasure Island*.

Picnic areas, hiking and nature trails and world class diving access are provided. Whale watching is also popular when the awesome animals pass close to shore on their 12,000-mile winter migration to Baja California. Hikers should be wary of poison oak.

Scenic Drive
★ **Scenic Road**
S for approximately 2 mi. from foot of Ocean Av.
Whether walking, bicycling, or driving, this aptly named street delights everyone who uses it. Through green tunnels created by overhanging branches of majestic pines, past tiny rockbound coves and white sand beaches, unusual residences and colorful flower gardens, the route follows the shoreline. Take a short detour along the way to 26304 Ocean View Avenue to visit **Tor House** and **Hawk Tower**, the home and refuge of Robinson Jeffers (a famous American poet). The drive ends at a panoramic viewpoint overlooking the mouth of Carmel River at the Pacific Ocean with the Big Sur beyond.

Spas
★ **Bernardus Lodge & Spa** *(831)658-3560*
11 mi. SE at 415 W. Carmel Valley Rd. - Carmel Valley
bernarduslodge.com
The Spa at Bernardus Lodge is a true haven of tranquility. Treatments of all kinds include specialties like the Valley Cascades (a lavender-infused Vichy steam treatment and a full body salve of decadent whipped shea butter). For the magic of romance, both of you are treated in a couples' suite to full-body exfoliation followed by an al fresco revitalizing bath culminated by an indulgent full-body warm-oil massage. The gracious warming room overlooks a firepit and a large warm outdoor soaking pool. Mens' and womens' facilities each feature a sauna and steam room, and spa visitors have access to the resort's large swimming pool surrounded by spectacular landscaping. There is also a full-service salon for hair and nail grooming. All day use of the resort's facilities is a major benefit of a treatment here. Also, the idyllic setting and lovely treatment rooms make this a fine getaway choice for a soothing couples massage or other modality.

★ **Carmel Valley Ranch** *(831)626-2586 (855)687-7262*
  8 mi. SE at 1 Old Ranch Rd. - Carmel Valley
  carmelvalleyranch.com
The Ranch's full-service **Spa Aiyana** offers guests 18 and older a wealth of massage and body therapy treatments as well as facials, skin care and a nail salon. Also available are oxygen infusion and body waxing. Many treatments feature lavender grown on site and worked by the Ranch's bee colony for services like lavender-honey nail care or foot massage. The spa facilities include a complete fitness center; steam and indoor/ outdoor relaxation chambers for both men and women with intimate oak views and a co-ed relaxation area; plus access to the large adult pool and an impressive infinity-edge whirlpool overlooking the golf course and oak forest. There is also a very complete spa shop.

★ **The Lodge at Pebble Beach** *(831)574-5574*
  3 mi. NW at 1700 Seventeen-Mile Dr. - Pebble Beach
  pebblebeach.com
The lodge's **Spa at Pebble Beach** is one of the most complete spa/relaxation facilities anywhere. Guests 18 or older either pay for day use of the amenities (free to Resort guests) or book a treatment which allows full facility usage. Each side (mens and womens) includes a whirlpool, sauna, eucalyptus steam room, oxygen-inhalation room (a quick, comfortable way to load up on negative ions), and first-rate relaxation rooms. Couples can get back together in the conservatory or by the firepit in the sanctuary. For an unusual spa treat for men or women, try the specialty "water experience" offered with a multi-jetted shower—a thrilling car wash for the body. The spa also has a courtyard pool, juice bar, and gift shop.

★ **Refuge** *(831)620-7360*
  4 mi. SE at 27300 Rancho San Carlos Rd. - Carmel Valley
  refuge.com
This unique experience is just the ticket to de-stress and totally refresh your body and your mind in a most enjoyable way. Using a "hydrothermal cycle," you start with a few minutes in a warm spacious eucalyptus steam room or a dry cedar sauna (the largest co-ed sauna in the country) to elevate your temperature. Next, dip (briefly) into a cold plunge. Then, relax in your choice of

any of the serene outdoor settings. After about three rounds, each ending with a distinctive different pool setting, you will feel a warm relaxed glow that normally comes after major exercise—but without the effort! The magical setting comes from the variety of ingeniously landscaped hot and cold pools, many with a babbling waterfall tumbling into the enclosure. The facilities can be rented for day use, or can be enjoyed as an adjunct to one of three massage treatments: Swedish, sports, or deep tissue. For optimal results, come ahead of your massage (book in advance to be sure of availability) and begin with the warming treatment. Ideally, refrain from alcohol but eat before your treatment. Bring a bathing suit because clothing is required; it's all co-ed except for changing rooms. No food or electronics are to be used on the premises, and quietude is respected, all contributing to the serenity. Note guests must be at least 18 years of age. Several firepits glowing in evening hours among the night-lighted warm and cold pools make evening use a particularly memorable experience. Open 10–10.

Wineries
  (831)375-9400   montereywines.org
Carmel Valley is an increasingly important source of vineyards in Monterey County—one of the largest producers of premium wine grapes in America. Wine tasting facilities are ubiquitous both in downtown Carmel and in Carmel Valley. Almost all charge a tasting fee. Many refund the fee if wine is purchased. A passport is available for downtown tasting rooms where a single fee covers tasting in most of them. Selected downtown restaurants will waive their corkage fee for wines purchased at the participating wineries.

★ **Downtown Tasting Rooms** *(the six most notable)*
  Caraccioli Cellars   *(831)622-7722*
  downtown at Dolores St. between Ocean & 7th Avs.
  caracciolicellars.com
Caraccioli Cellars makes the only methode sparkling wine (champagne) on the Peninsula, and they are doing a good job with classic emphasis on pinot noir and on chardonnay. Still wines are also available for tastes in the sophisticated little tasting room with padded stools and Reidel crystal for all pours. Open 2–7 or 8, longer on weekends (hours vary).

Dawn's Dream   *(831)659-2649*
downtown at NW corner of 7th Av. & San Carlos St.
dawnsdreamwinery.com
Chardonnay and pinot noirs are notable in a cheerful spacious tasting room outfitted with whimsical art objects with a light bright touch. A cheese plate is available. Success of Dawn's Dream with award-winning premium wines has resulted in a business model that allows the owners the opportunity to "live the dream" and give back to organizations helping those less fortunate. Open daily 12–6, and 12–7 on Sat.

Figge Tasting Bar   *(831)233-0483*
downtown on Dolores between Ocean & 7th Av.
figgecellars.com
Figge Cellars has a tiny tasting area of only half a dozen stools at a freeform polished wood counter near the entrance to a major gallery. Two kinds of both pinot noirs and chardonnays are excellent examples of the quality that noble grapes are achieving in the wine-growing reaches near Carmel. Open Wed.–Mon. noon–close. Closed Tues.

Galante Vineyards Tasting Room   *(831)624-3800*
downtown on Dolores between Ocean & 7th Avs.
galantevineyards.com   *(800)425-2683*
Owner Jack Galante's great grandfather was the founder of the town of Carmel. Jack started growing premium cabernet sauvignon grapes in 1983 on their cattle ranch and built a winery in 1995. Today Galante consistently produces some of the finest local estate-grown wines in California. Their flagship, "Blackjack Pasture" cabernet sauvignon, is one of America's truly great wines. The delightful tucked-away tasting room in the heart of Carmel is open 1–6 except 12–7 on Sat.

Manzoni   *(831)620-6541*
downtown between Ocean & 7th Avs. at 416 San Carlos St.
manzoniwines.com
Tucked away in a colorful garden court, this family winery has a handsome polished-wood bar and notable pinot noir and pinot noir reserve. Chardonnay is also worth discovering, as is the pinot gris in the little tasting room with half a dozen seats. Open 11–6 (later occasionally).

Silvestri Vineyards *(831)625-0111*
downtown on 7th Av. between Dolores & San Carlos Sts.
silvestrivineyards.com
Alan Silvestri, a major motion picture music composer, is now
also passionate about fine wines. Estate bottlings of chardonnay
and pinot noir are award winners in this family-owned winery
with an attractive tasting room in downtown Carmel. Open
12–7 daily.

★ **Wineries in Carmel Valley** *(the seven most notable)*
  Bernardus Vineyards & Winery *(831)298-8021*
  13 mi. SE at 5 W. Carmel Valley Rd. - Carmel Valley
  bernardus.com (800)223-2533
A simply sophisticated tasting room has provisions for various
levels of tasting indoors and on an umbrella-shaded patio. The
"Ingrid" chardonnay and pinot noir are the specialty results
of grapes grown adjacent to the resort. Open 11–5 daily.
  Boekenoogen Wines *(831)659-4215*
  13 mi. SE at 24 W. Carmel Valley Rd. - Carmel Valley
  boekenoogenwines.com
Here is an unusual name worth remembering. This relatively
small producer's estate-grown premium wines are consistently fine examples of their varietals. The pinot noirs are
especially notable and the viognier is one of the best of its
kind in California. The tasting room is comfortably furnished
with tables and chairs where you can enjoy premium wines.
Open 11–5 daily.
  Folktale Winery & Vineyards *(831)293-7500*
  7 mi. SE at 8940 Carmel Valley Rd. - Carmel Valley
  folktalewinery.com
One of Carmel Valley's longest-established wineries became
Folktale in 2015. The French chateau-inspired winery is being
transformed into a contemporary mode where renovations
and changes will reflect the new owner's interest in providing
a creative and social space as well as wines. Guests receive a
complimentary sparkling brut on arrival. All sorts of tastes are
available, with or without food, scheduled tours (reservations
encouraged), and frequent special events and live music. Formal
gardens and lawn games further reflect the cheerful warmth of
this 21st century take on winery hospitality. Open 11–8 daily.

Georis Winery Tasting Room   *(831)659-1080*
13 mi. SE at 1 Pilot Rd. - Carmel Valley
georiswine.com
Beyond a garden setting and a dramatic stained-glass entrance wall, this relatively new location for one of the Valley's oldest (and one of the most notable) premium wine producers is doing consistently fine work with several wines. Don't miss the chardonnay and the sauvignon blanc, in addition to reds (cabernet franc, pinot noir and merlot blend) which have deservedly won major awards. Also, various levels of flights are available with food as well as wine by the glass at comfortable seated locations. Open Mon.–Thurs. 11:30–5, Fri.–Sun. 11:30–6.

Heller Estate   *(831)659-6220   (800)625-8466*
13 mi. SE at 69 W. Carmel Valley Rd. - Carmel Valley
hellerestate.com
Heller Estate was the region's first grower of premium varietals. All of their wines from organically grown grapes are available for tastings in a handsome roadside shop with an adjoining sculpture garden with tables and chairs for picnics. They also sell their jam from organically grown fruits. Open 11–5:30 daily.

Parsonage   *(831)659-7322*
13 mi. SE at 19 E. Carmel Valley Rd. - Carmel Valley
parsonagewine.com
Red wines shine at Parsonage. Their syrah is the most notable of the variety in the region, and the cabernet sauvignon and pinot noir are also fine. The appealing little tasting room is backed by some wall art that includes colorful quilts and quilt images used for the label logo. Open 11–5 daily.

Talbott Vineyards   *(831)659-3500*
13 mi. SE at 25 Pilot Rd. - Carmel Valley
talbottvineyards.com
Following a long evolution, Talbott is selectively now among the producers of fine estate-bottled premium wine. Especially notable is Diamond T Vineyard where very limited bottlings of both chardonnay and pinot noir are excellent, especially noted for the terroir. There is a very large tasting room and expansive patios with picnic tables on either side are well suited to showcasing Talbott's products. Open 11–5 daily.

RESTAURANTS

★ **Andre's Bouchée**   *(831)626-7880*
downtown at Mission St. between Ocean & 7th Avs.
andresbouchee.com
L–D. No L Mon.–Thurs.   *Expensive*
Bouchée is one of the Peninsula's well-rated restaurants. For the modern bistro menu, the Parisian-born chef features seasonal local provisions in contemporary French cuisine with a California coastal flair. Plush, fully-linened tables are lined up in an intimate, mod dining room with a wine shop.

★ **Anton & Michel**   *(831)624-2406*
downtown on Mission St. between Ocean & 7th Avs.
antonandmichel.com
L–D.   *Expensive*
In this long-established restaurant, contemporary California cuisine now holds forth with dishes ranging from lamb chops to sand dabs. Elegant dining rooms give guests a choice of romantic firelight or courtyard fountain views. The firelit lounge includes plush sofa seating and an appealing small-bites menu.

★ **A. W. Shucks Cocktail & Oyster Bar**   *(831)624-6605*
downtown on Ocean Av. between San Carlos & Dolores Sts.
awshuckscarmel.com
L–D.   *Moderate*
This young restaurant is already a major crowd pleaser with skilled attention paid to a thoughtful limited selection of contemporary California favorites. For starters, consider steamed artichoke, or a choice of New England (white) or Manhattan (red) clam chowder, or rose (a special blend of both). Follow it up with beer-batter jumbo prawns and chips, or the house specialty, fresh cold water oysters on the half shell. It's all done simply with finesse including desserts like a homemade key lime pie. The long narrow dining room also contributes to the happy hubbub.

★ **Basil**   *(831)626-8226*
downtown on San Carlos between Ocean & 7th Avs.
basilcarmel.com
L–D. Sun. brunch.   *Expensive*
Classic California contemporary cuisine is given skilled attention in dishes that feature seasonally fresh local ingredients.

Consider a small plate of local Monterey abalone, or Castroville artichoke salad. Dinner entrees might include grilled Niman Ranch pork chop, or duck breast with mushrooms and spinach in puff pastry. Chef-made desserts also reflect classic training and an adventurous spirit in unusual treats like Fuji apple strudel with figs and pine nuts with vanilla sauce. The small mod dining room is enhanced by a heated little garden court dining area.

★ **Bernardus Lodge & Spa**   *(831)658-3400*
   11 mi. SE at 415 Carmel Valley Rd. - Carmel Valley
   bernarduslodge.com/wine-cuisine
   B–L–D.   *Very Expensive*
Lucia Restaurant & Lounge is the landmark dining room of the Bernardus Lodge. Here, one of Monterey Peninsula's legendary chefs has for years overseen the meticulous creation of traditional and innovative California country cuisine. Top-quality seasonally fresh products of the region enhanced by the resort's extensive gardens of herbs, vegetables and vineyards of chardonnay and pinot noir grapes complement the kitchen's talent with foie gras and other gourmet ingredients. The pastry chef also prepares desserts of the season that are as decadent as they are beautiful. Housemade ice cream features changing innovative flavors like basil, and the semifreddo (when available) is sublime. The dining room showcases casually elegant country decor with widely spaced tables and booths, raised stone fireplace and a window-wall view past a firelit dining deck to premium vineyards. Another dining deck (for breakfast and lunch only) overlooks gardens and a green grass games area.

★ **Cafe Rustica**   *(831)659-4444*
   13 mi. SE at 10 Del Fino Place - Carmel Valley
   caferusticavillage.com
   L–D. Closed Wed.   *Moderate*
Contemporary California cuisine derived from all sorts of Continental specialties is skillfully prepared for dishes like fresh steamed clams, grilled salmon filet and assorted thin-crust pizzas and pastas. For dessert, try country apple galette or fresh lemon pudding cake with strawberries. Dining areas with stone floors, rock walls and polished hardwood tables and chairs and a heated patio carry off the warm rustic theme.

★ **Carmel Bakery**   *(831)626-8885*
downtown on Ocean Av. between Dolores & Lincoln Sts.
carmelbakery.com
B–L–D.   *Moderate*
In Carmel's longest-established retail business, Carmel Bakery has been the village's main source of baked goods for well over a century. Nowadays, delicious morning delights like sticky buns, cinnamon rolls, bagels and raspberry sticks or several kinds of croissants can be enjoyed with assorted hot beverages at tables near loaded display cases. Several kinds of big soft pretzels star later along with designer sandwiches using bread baked on-site.

★ **Carmel Belle**   *(831)624-1600*
downtown on San Carlos between Ocean & 7th Avs.
carmelbelle.com
B–L–D. No D Mon. & Tues.   *Moderate*
Carmel Belle is deservedly popular for its tempting chalkboard menu of traditional and au courant California dishes. Organic treats range from roasted mushroom melt; mixed green walnut, apple and blue cheese salad; free-range chicken pot pie; to a local-catch dinner with seasonal sides like grilled local asparagus. Chalkboard orders are served to a casual coffee shop or an inviting big back dining area with padded booths or chairs, and an open fireplace. Specialty pastries and luscious desserts made here are displayed and sold at an adjoining counter.

★ **Carmel Valley Ranch**   *(831)626-2599*
8 mi. SE at 1 Old Ranch Rd.
carmelvalleyranch.com
B–L–D.   *Very Expensive*
At the heart of the resort, **Valley Kitchen** features creative California cuisine in breakfast palate-pleasers like ricotta pancakes and applewood-smoked bacon. For dinner, consider fried sea salt shishito peppers as an appetizer, along with Dungeness crabcake, pizza, or Black Angus filet. In the main dining room, guests can enjoy picture-window wall views on one side, a stone fireplace and a large handsome post-mod bar and lounge plus comfortable wicker armchair seating overlooking the pool.

★ **Casanova Restaurant** *(831)625-0501*
downtown on 5th Av. between Mission & San Carlos Sts.
casanovarestaurant.com
L–D.   *Very Expensive*
Casanova Restaurant is one of Carmel's best and most enduring
special-occasion destinations. Classic French and Italian cuisine
receives creative California topspin showcasing fresh regional
ingredients. Consider dishes like fettuccine with lobster, clam,
mussels and prawn, or rack of lamb. Homemade desserts
are also inspired. Romantic dining adventures for adults are
enjoyed in a series of intimate dining rooms around a heated
garden patio.

★ **Christopher's** *(831)626-8000*
downtown on Lincoln between 5th & 6th
christophersrestaurantcarmel.com
D only.   *Expensive*
Contemporary California cuisine is given expert attention
in dishes ranging from cornmeal-crusted spicy chile rellano
with rock shrimp through entrees like pan-seared breast of
Muscovy duck to distinctive housemade desserts. In the split-
level dining room, pleasant quiet music, a fireplace, interesting
wine-related wall art, and tables set with full linen provide a
romantic backdrop.

Corkscrew Cafe *(831)659-8888*
13 mi. SE at 55 W. Carmel Valley Rd. - Carmel Valley
corkscrewcafe.com
L–D. Closed Tues.   *Expensive*
A limited selection of appetizers, salads, entrees, and side dishes
ranges from wood-fired whole trout to spiced Maple Leaf duck
or seafood stew. Delectable desserts might include chocolate
malted cake. The small dining room reflects an easygoing refined
rusticity enhanced by an impressive collection of corkscrews
and other wine-related paraphernalia.

★ **The Cottage Restaurant** *(831)625-6260*
downtown on Lincoln St. between Ocean & 7th Avs.
cottagerestaurant.com
B–L.   *Moderate*
The Cottage is serious competition for the best omelet on the
Peninsula. Select three from a list of 20 ingredients for your

omelet and they will skillfully transform them and serve them with tasty skin-on cottage potatoes. All sorts of other traditional American light fare are served at breakfast and lunch in a cottage with a quaint interior outfitted with wooden booths or bentwood chairs in rooms enhanced by picture-window views of downtown and local wall hangings and objects of art.

★ **Dametra Cafe** *(831)622-7766*
downtown at Ocean Av. at Lincoln St.
dametracafe.com
L–D. *Moderate*
Perhaps the most auspicious of the Peninsula's current foodie phenoms is Dametra. Dishes representing most Mediterranean nations are skillfully prepared, attractively presented, and fairly priced. All cater to an audience that clearly includes both locals and visitors. A cozy congestion of tables fills a room made warm and cheerful by some excellent murals, nifty decor touches, and a handsome small bar. Every hour and a half or so, talented staff entertains with a robust performance of Continental songs.

★ **Flaherty's Seafood Grill & Oyster Bar** *(831)625-1500*
downtown on 6th Av. between Dolores & San Carlos Sts.
flahertyseafood.com
L–D. *Expensive*
A notably diverse selection of seafood is topped by specials for fish available seasonally throughout the year. West Coast specialties ranging from kumomoto oysters to red or white clam or crab chowder or lobster bisque, to sea bass or sand dabs have been featured in the Grill (for dinner) and the oyster bar (lunch or dinner) since 1975. Homemade pies (especially a refreshing key lime) and other desserts are additional reasons to be here. A light bright little room's casual congested lunch counter has plain, closely spaced tables, and a more comfortable adjoining dining room is also used at dinner.

★ **Flying Fish Grill** *(831)625-1962*
downtown at Carmel Plaza (on Mission bet. Ocean & 7th)
flyingfishgrill.com
D only. *Expensive*
Innovative Asian-inspired cuisine is featured in dishes like sesame salmon or almond sea bass or beef clay pots cooked at

your table, and in desserts like a green tea sundae. Ginger salsa and chips that begin each meal are an unusual and delightful beginning for the creative tasteful dishes to follow. The simply sophisticated wood-trim cellar restaurant is enhanced by a wealth of whimsical art. Several small firelit dining rooms provide an intimate comfortable setting for some of the Peninsula's finest cuisine.

The Forge in the Forest *(831)624-2233*
downtown at 5th Av. & Junipero St.
forgeintheforest.com
L–D.   *Expensive*
One of Carmel's venerable watering holes features an ornate wooden bar in a saloon with nostalgic blacksmith antiques and intriguing copper walls that gleam in the light of the room's fireplace. A tasty pub menu is served. Outside is a classic-Carmel lush garden patio with a four-side stone fireplace.

Friar Tuck's Restaurant   *(831)624-4274*
downtown at Dolores St. & 5th Av.
friartucksrestaurant.com
B–L.   *Expensive*
Traditional American fare is offered including a wide variety of omelets for breakfast served in a casually comfortable little dining room with a corner window view of downtown.

★ **Grasing's**   *(831)624-6562*
downtown at 6th Av. & Mission St.
grasings.com
L–D.   *Very Expensive*
Coastal cuisine achieves landmark status in Grasing's, a Carmel showcase in dishes like Maple Leaf duck with fresh cherries, heritage pork medallions, or milk-fed veal chop. Housemade desserts are delicious, too, like almond cake with raspberry coulis, or lemon tart. Wall art and town-and-garden-view windows enhance romantic dining areas upscaled with linen and candles, and there is an intimate heated shaded garden courtyard.

The Grill on Ocean Avenue   *(831)624-2569*
downtown on Ocean Av. between Lincoln & Dolores Sts.
thegrillcarmel.com
L–D.   *Expensive*

An oakwood-fired grill is used for an eclectic menu with attention to local ingredients. Consider grilled Castroville artichoke or Monterey Bay sand dabs. The relaxed but stylish firelit dining room complements the cuisine.

Hog's Breath Inn   *(831)625-1044*
downtown off San Carlos St. between 5th & 6th Avs.
hogsbreathinn.net
L–D.   Expensive
The California pub grub hasn't changed much in more than forty years in Clint Eastwood's one-time watering hole. Castroville artichoke dip, baby back ribs, and seasonal fruit cobbler with oatmeal strudel are examples. Neither has decor like a rustic little bar with a corner fireplace; or the more-polished dining room featuring more fireplaces and images of Clint. The courtyard features hogs in sculptures and a colorful full-wall mural of a Carmel Valley scene toward Big Sur.

★ **Hyatt Carmel Highlands**   *(831)622-5445*
6 mi. S (on Highway 1) at 120 Highlands Dr. - Big Sur
pacificsedge.com
B–L–D.   Very Expensive
The resort's superbly-sited **Pacific's Edge Restaurant** (D only) was renovated in May 2016 and features seasonally fresh local and organic ingredients. Contemporary California dishes ranging from Monterey Bay red abalone appetizer or wild mushroom soup to wild Pacific king salmon have to compete with one of America's great dining room views. An expansive three-level dining room features floor-to-ceiling window-wall views on two sides of the Big Sur landscape and surf crashing against headlands far below in the Pacific Ocean. Nearby, a plush firelit lounge shares the romantic seascape, and features live grand piano music. The more casual **California Market** (B-L) moved in mid-2016 to a larger site with some ocean view.

★ **The Inn at Spanish Bay**   *(831)647-7433*
6 mi. N at 2700 Seventeen-Mile Dr. - Pebble Beach
pebblebeach.com
L–D.   Very Expensive
At **Pèppoli at Pebble Beach** (D only—Very Expensive), contemporary California cuisine is skillfully prepared in dishes ranging from king salmon to filet mignon. The casually elegant

---

main dining room has a window wall on two sides providing an inspiring panorama of Pacific Ocean surf crashing against the coast beyond. **Traps** is a clubby evening lounge with a surf view. **Roy's** (L–D—Very Expensive) local representative of the upscale chain features a wealth of Hawaiian and Asian style sushi and entrees like hibachi salmon. The posh dining room has a full ocean view beyond a window wall on two sides. **Sticks** (B–L–D—Expensive), adjacent to a putting course and tennis court and Olympic pool, is a good source for upscale pub grub of all sorts and impressive desserts.

Jeffrey's Grill & Catering *(831)624-2029*
8 mi. E at 112 Mid-Valley Center - Carmel Valley
jeffreysgrillandcatering.com
B–L. Closed Mon. *Moderate*
Jeffrey's is a good bet for breakfasts like seasonal berry pancakes or a designer omelet, or deep-fried apple fritters with choice of spicy sausage, bacon or ham, plus assorted housemade muffins. Homemade desserts are on display, too. The cheerful coffee shop and adjoining dining deck overlook colorful gardens.

Katy's Place *(831)624-0199*
downtown on Mission St. between 5th & 6th Avs.
katysplacecarmel.com
B–L. *Expensive*
Eggs benedict (20+ kinds) are the specialty at Katy's, but there are also contemporary California dishes ranging from bay shrimp omelets to buttermilk or oatmeal pancakes, pecan waffles, french toast and more. Diners have a choice of seating at the counter; in the dining room; or (a clear favorite on a nice day) the redwood-shaded heated dining deck by a picturesque downtown street.

★ **La Balena** *(831)250-6295*
downtown on Junipero between 5th & 6th Avs.
labalenacarmel.com
L–D. No L Tues. & Wed. Closed Mon. *Very Expensive*
A limited menu of Italian specialties is offered. Every dish reflects skilled attention to seasonally fresh ingredients. The tucked-away restaurant features intimate atmospheric dining rooms and a lush heated outdoor courtyard shaded by a large handsome redwood and overhead awnings.

★ **La Bicyclette** *(831)622-9899*
downtown at Dolores St. & 7th Av.
labicycletterestaurant.com
B–L–D.   *Expensive*
"Rustic European family style cuisine" is skillfully prepared
with careful attention to detail for year-round seasonal dining
using local farm ingredients like organic free-range eggs, plus
housemade sausages and jams and 100% maple syrup. A short
list of housemade breads and pastries includes croissants,
turnovers, scones and artisan sourdough loaves. The dinner
menu is similarly engaging with dishes like wood-fired escargot
and mariner's stew featuring mussels and petrale sole plus
assorted wood-fired oven pizzas. Wood-trimmed tables and
chairs in two dining areas are surrounded by massive artful
cabinets, clerestory window views of downtown and a small
handsome always-busy kitchen and wood-fired oven to complete
the view.

★ **Little Napoli** *(831)626-6335*
downtown at Dolores St. & 7th Av.
littlenapoli.com
L–D.   *Expensive*
Traditional Italian bistro dishes are featured in housemade
spicy sausage, cannelloni tri-colore, or black mussels in tomato
broth. Skillfully prepared contemporary California options
include cedar-planked Pacific Northwest salmon. Luscious
desserts made here range from classics like tiramisu to house
specialties like limoncello mousse cake. Hardwood tables and
chairs are surrounded by a wealth of colorful Napoli-style
pictures and art objects. There is also a romantic little courtyard
dining patio. Next door, **Vino Napoli** showcases a changing
selection of local wines by the taste or glass with assorted
appetizers. A limited assortment of salads and pizzas is also
served in the stylish bistro barroom with fireplaces and views
of downtown Carmel.

★ **Lodge at Pebble Beach** *(831)622-8756*
3 mi. NW at 1700 Seventeen-Mile Dr. - Pebble Beach
pebblebeach.com
B–L–D. Sun. brunch.   *Expensive–Very Expensive*
Stillwater Bar & Grill (B–L–D. Sun. brunch—Very Expensive)

features fresh seafood and farm specialties of the region amid casual elegance. **The Tap Room** (L–D—Expensive) features steaks, chops and salmon and more casual fare like meatloaf served in armchaired comfort in a handsome club-style lounge. **The Bench** (L–D—Expensive) offers au courant California fare in creations like duck-fat potatoes with truffles or black mussels with chili-lime broth and chilies, or assorted designer flatbreads or blistered shishito peppers. Beyond the large barroom there is a lower-level dining area and an outdoor terrace. All overlook the legendary golf course with ocean surf beyond and Point Lobos in the distance.

★ **Mission Ranch**   *(831)625-9040*
1 mi. S at 26270 Dolores St.
missionranchcarmel.com
D only. Sun. brunch.   *Expensive*
The **Restaurant at Mission Ranch** skillfully pairs a historic century-old ranch house with contemporary California dishes with roots going way back. Consider locally grown artichoke or smoked salmon appetizer. Among entrees, the big slab of roast prime rib of beef, baby back ribs, or New York strip steak are fine. The firelit dining room and adjoining lounge with nightly grand piano bar entertainment exude Carmel conviviality. Just below, a heated dining deck shares the delightful view of the bucolic Carmel River mouth and nearby Big Sur Mountains.

Patisserie Boissiere   *(831)624-5008*
downtown at Carmel Plaza on Mission St. near Ocean Av.
patisserieboissiere.com
L–D. Sat. & Sun. brunch. No D Mon. & Tues.   *Moderate*
For many years, pastries, cakes, tarts, and breads from their bakery have been served with light meals with a Continental flair in a French country-charming firelit dining room. Lunch and dinners feature regional specialties with French and Continental topspins in dishes like artichoke vinaigrette and assorted housemade Continental-style desserts. They also offer a menu for takeout picnics.

Rio Grill   *(831)625-5436*
1 mi. SE at 101 Crossroads Blvd. (in the Crossroads)
riogrill.com
L–D.   *Expensive*

Rio Grill was an early source of New California cuisine. While the cast has changed, emphasis is still on local sourcing and innovative preparation. Avant-garde art enlivens a series of cheerful Santa Fe-style alcoves beyond a colorful firelit bar.

Robata Grill & Sake Bar   *(831)624-2643*
1 mi. SE at 3658 The Barnyard
robata-barnyard.com
L–D. Closed Sun.   *Moderate*
The long-established restaurant gives careful attention to classic and creative Japanese dishes from sushi to green tea ice cream. Polished redwood tops a dramatic sushi bar which enhances dining areas and a heated courtyard.

Roux Restaurant   *(831)659-5020*
13 mi. SE at 6 Pilot Rd. - Carmel Valley
rouxcarmel.com
L–D. Closed Mon. except in summer.   *Expensive*
New in 2016, a French chef has mixed Gallic and contemporary California cuisine featuring seasonally fresh local ingredients. Little dining areas and an outdoor tree-shaded deck and garden patio capture the spirit of the south of France. Come in the morning for fresh-made beignets (including tasty strawberry and other fillings) and coffee.

Tommy's Wok   *(831)624-8518*
downtown on San Carlos between Ocean & 7th Avs.
tommyswokcarmel.com
L–D. Closed Mon.   *Moderate*
Tommy's, tucked away in a courtyard, has won acclaim for some distinctive dishes like rainbow seafood chowder and seaweed soup. Also, consider a flaming pu pu platter for two or cheese crab puffs with sweet and sour sauce and entrees like broccoli beef or mu shu pork. A casual usually busy little dining room contributes to the happy hubbub generated by Tommy's popular takes on Szechwan, Hunan and Mandarin cuisine.

Tuck Box   *(831)624-6365*
downtown on Dolores St. between Ocean & 7th Avs.
tuckbox.com
B–L.   *Expensive*
The Tuck Box has been a Carmel tradition for more than half a century. The thatched cottage facade of the tiny English tea

room is very photogenic. The interior showcases their own scone mix and preserves in a cozy, unassuming little tea shop.

Vesuvio *(831)625-1766*
   downtown at Junipero St. & 6th Av.
   vesuviocarmel.com
   D only.   *Expensive*
Traditional and creative Italian cuisine is given expert attention on a menu that is very similar to Little Napoli. A split-level dining room is comfortably outfitted with hardwood tables and padded chairs surrounded by numerous large wall hanging photos from Italy and a forty-foot-long floor-to-ceiling mural reflecting the sophistication of Roman-style painting.

Village Corner *(831)624-3588*
   downtown at 6th Av. & Dolores St.
   villagecornerbistro.com
   B–L–D.   *Expensive*
Banana pecan pancakes are featured along with waffles, french toast, plus omelets for breakfast. Light California fare is prepared over an oak-fired open grill in this pleasant Mediterranean-style coffee shop with a heated garden court.

Wagon Wheel Coffee Shop *(831)624-8878*
   5 mi. SE at 7156 Carmel Valley Rd. - Carmel Valley
   B–L.   *Moderate*
Omelets, biscuits and gravy, or banana-pecan pancakes are highlights in this long-popular outpost. A cozy congestion of tables surrounds an expo kitchen in casual dining areas amidst a passel of Western memorabilia.

Yafa *(0624-9232*
   downtown at Junipero St. & 5th Av.
   yafarestaurant.com
   D only.   *Moderate*
Eastern Mediterranean dishes are featured, ranging from lamb ravioli to assorted specialty meat kabobs plus American classics like petrale sole or salmon. Closely spaced tables topped by colorful vinyl tablecloths, wall hangings and artifacts of the Middle Eastern region and frequent live music contribute to conviviality.

LODGINGS

Lodgings in Carmel are abundant, small-scale, individualistic, and invariably picturesque. Renowned resorts surround the village. High season rates top out in May through October, and daily rates are highest on Friday and Saturday year-round. In winter, rates may be as much as 20% less mid-week.

★ **Bernardus Lodge & Spa**   *(831)658-3400*
11 mi. SE at 415 W. Carmel Valley Rd. (Box 80) - Carmel Valley 93924
bernarduslodge.com
73 units   *Very Expensive*
Bernardus is a splendid resort sequestered among oaks and pines on a gentle slope of the Carmel River Valley. In this romantic adult hideaway, a luxuriant chardonnay and pinot noir vineyard lies just beyond beautiful gardens that surround contemporary California-style low-rise buildings, two tennis courts, a large outdoor pool, and professional-class bocce ball and croquet courts. Guests have full use of additional facilities in the exceptional spa (see listing) and salon. The main lodge includes gourmet dining (see listing). A glass of their distinguished wine (see listing) is offered at check-in, and every room is stocked with a generous complimentary welcome package including wine and snacks. Each spacious unit is individually luxuriously furnished and includes a refrigerator; gas fireplace; two-person soaking tub and spacious walk-in shower; and large balcony or deck with a view of gardens and mountains beyond.
      #1, #6—extra-large, all of the above features
            plus a large whirlpool in the private patio.
      Suites and Villas (14 of these)—open summer 2016,
            extra-large one- and two-bedroom units
            with expansive views of vineyards.

★ **Candlelight Inn**   *(831)624-6451*   *(800)832-3224*
downtown on San Carlos St. bet. 4th & 5th (Box 101) - 93921
innsbythesea.com
20 units   *Expensive*
The Candlelight Inn is a motel that has been delightfully updated and upscaled. The beautifully landscaped grounds include an unusual garden court firepit. Complimentary Continental breakfast basket is delivered each morning and cookies are available every afternoon. Each unit is well furnished and

includes a refrigerator. Some have a microwave or kitchenette.
#14, #15—spacious with raised Duraflame fireplace,
big two-person raised whirlpool in separate
room with louvered doors open to bedroom.

Carmel Bay View Inn - Best Western Plus   *(831)624-1831*
downtown on Junipero St. bet. 5th & 6th (Box 3715) - 93921
carmelbayviewinn.com
59 units   Moderate–Expensive
A large courtyard pool and expanded complimentary Continental
breakfast are features of Carmel's largest motel. All rooms in
the contemporary five-story complex are attractively furnished
and include a refrigerator. Many have a gas fireplace.
"Deluxe View Room" (several)—beautifully furnished,
gas fireplace, private distant-ocean-view balcony.

Carmel Country Inn   *(831)625-3263   (800)215-6343*
just N at Dolores St. & 3rd Av. (Box 3756) - 93921
carmelcountryinn.com
12 units   Expensive–Very Expensive
Tucked away at the far north end of the commercial area
is a well-maintained older inn built into luxuriant gardens.
Continental breakfast and afternoon snacks and cookies are
complimentary. Each well-furnished room has a refrigerator.
Treetop—raised gas fireplace and one-person whirlpool
in view of fireplace and large balcony with treescape.

★ **Carmel Garden Inn**   *(831)624-6926   (888)514-9640*
downtown on 4th Av. at Torres St. (Box 5547) - 93921
carmelgardeninn.com
10 units   Expensive
The epitome of the Carmel spirit is showcased in this artistic
small inn. Homemade breakfast with a hot dish is presented
each morning, and there are appetizers and wine tasting in the
afternoon. Units in the complex are surrounded by luxuriant
subtropical and Northern California vegetation flowering year-
round. Both the meticulous landscaping and the attractively
furnished rooms contribute to an adult sanctuary feel. Each
room has a full separate kitchenette and best of all, a wood-
burning fireplace.

Carmel Mission Inn   *(831)624-1841   (800)348-9090*
1 mi. SE (off Highway 1) at 3665 Rio Rd. - 93923

carmelmissioninn.com
165 units   *Expensive–Very Expensive*
The Mission, Barnyard, and Crossroad shops are a stroll from Carmel Valley's largest full-service hotel. The four-story contemporary complex has a garden pool, whirlpool, fitness center, restaurant and lounge. Each well-furnished room has a refrigerator. Some also have a private patio or balcony.

★ **Carmel Valley Ranch**   *(831)625-9500*   *(866)282-4745*
    8 mi. SE (via Carmel Valley Rd.) at 1 Old Ranch Rd. - 93923
    carmelvalleyranch.com
    181 units   *Very Expensive*
Carmel Valley Ranch is a delightful California hideaway resort. Noble oak trees shade the grounds of this exclusive adult playground high on a hill overlooking a Shangri-La valley a few miles from the ocean. A wealth of resort activities is available, including an educational (fee) "Bee Experience;" or horseback riding. Amenities include **Spa Aiyana** (see listing), an 18-hole championship golf course, restaurant (see listing), nine tennis courts, hiking trails, a fitness center, steam room, two large adult pools and a family pool, and two whirlpools. Each spacious, luxuriously furnished suite has a refrigerator, gas fireplace, and a private deck with a pastoral valley view. Many also have a large in-bath or on-deck soaking tub.

    "Ranch King Suite"—large bedroom with gas
            fireplace and window-wall valley view;
            living room; bathroom with soaking tub
            and shower; big private deck with grand
            valley view from soaking tub.
    "Santa Lucia Studio Suites" (39 of these)—one
            large room, some have outdoor soaking
            tub and gas fireplace visible from deck.

★ **Carriage House Inn**   *(831)625-2585*   *(800)832-3224*
    downtown on Junipero St. bet. 7th & 8th (Box 1900) - 93921
    carriagehouseinncarmel.com
    13 units   *Very Expensive*
Carriage House Inn, which has long been one of California's most romantic bed-and-breakfast inns, was fully upgraded in 2015. The charming adult retreat in a garden captures the spirit of Carmel in quality arts and crafts and thoughtful

embellishments. Expanded Continental breakfast, afternoon wine and appetizers, and evening treats are served. Each spacious, luxuriously furnished room has a compact refrigerator with complimentary juice and water, and either a one- or two-person whirlpool tub or an in-bath "air" tub (larger than a regular tub and with air bubbles from the tub floor), and a gas fireplace.

> #3, #2—extra-large, in-bath two-person whirlpool, gas fireplace in sight of canopy bed.

Coachman's Inn   *(831)624-6421   (800)336-6421*
downtown at San Carlos St. & 7th Av. (Box C-1) - 93921
coachmansinn.com
30 units   *Expensive–Very Expensive*
Old English pleasantries and contemporary conveniences blend comfortably in a little complex with a whirlpool, sauna, and Continental breakfast, wine and appetizers, and cookies. Each spacious, well-furnished room has a refrigerator and microwave.

Colonial Terrace Inn   *(831)624-2741   (800)345-8220*
1 mi. SW on San Antonio at 13th Av. (Box 1375) - 93921
colonialterrace.com
28 units   *Expensive*
Located in a quiet residential area, this small romantic inn is comprised of several buildings (circa 1925) amid luxuriant garden terraces. It is an easy stroll from the ocean and a sugar-sand beach. Continental breakfast and afternoon cookies are complimentary. Each well-furnished unit is individually decorated. Some have a refrigerator. Most have a gas fireplace.

★ **Cypress Inn**   *(831)624-3871   (800)443-7443*
downtown at Lincoln St. & 7th Av. (Box Y) - 93921
cypress-inn.com
33 units   *Expensive–Very Expensive*
The lovely little Cypress Inn, a landmark since 1929 with a brilliant white facade and Spanish-tiled roof, is built around a garden courtyard. A fruit basket, sherry, and expanded Continental breakfast are complimentary. Gracious **Terry's Restaurant and Lounge** is surrounded by posters of one of the owners, Doris Day whose love of animals has made this a top dog destination. Each room is individually beautifully furnished.

Happy Landing Inn   *(831)624-7917*
downtown on Monte Verde bet. 5th & 6th (Box 2619) - 93921
carmelhappylanding.com
7 units   *Expensive–Very Expensive*
This small bed-and-breakfast inn is distinguished by a garden
setting and a 100% dog-friendly attitude. Each individually
attractively furnished room honors an American icon.
The Hideaway   *(831)625-5222*
downtown on Junipero St. & 8th Avs. (Box 3185) - 93921
hideawaycarmel.com
24 units   *Expensive*
Opened as The Hideaway in 2016, this property offers sleek
contemporary comfort an easy stroll from downtown Carmel
on the quiet side. Amenities include complimentary buffet-
style Continental breakfast, afternoon wine and appetizers,
and cookies. Each room is beautifully furnished and has a
refrigerator. Most have a raised gas fireplace.
Hofsas House   *(831)624-2745   (800)221-2548*
downtown at 4th Av. & San Carlos St. (Box 1195) - 93921
hofsashouse.com
37 units   *Moderate*
Amenities include a complimentary Continental breakfast and
a large kidney-shaped pool. Many of the attractively furnished
European-style rooms have a view over the pines and village
to the distant ocean. Some have a kitchenette, gas fireplace
and private balcony.
Horizon Inn/Ocean View Lodge   *(831)624-5327*
downtown at Junipero St. & 3rd Av. (Box 1693) - 93921
horizoninncarmel.com   (800)350-7723
26 units   *Expensive*
Fine distant ocean views are a feature of this motel-and-cottage
complex. A breakfast basket (Continental) delivered to the
room and use of an outdoor whirlpool are complimentary. Each
well-furnished room has a refrigerator and microwave. Some
rooms have a gas fireplace, one- or two-person whirlpool tub
and/or ocean view.
Hotel Carmel   *(831)293-6102*
downtown at 4th Av. & San Carlos St. (Box 7489) - 93923
thehotelcarmel.com

27 units   *Expensive–Very Expensive*
Complimentary Continental breakfast and whirlpool are
amenities at this upgraded motel, and there is an on-site
restaurant. Each room is well furnished and has a refrigerator.
★ **Hyatt Carmel Highlands**   *(831)620-1234*
  6 mi. S (on Highway 1) at 120 Highlands Dr. - 93923
  hyattcarmelhighlands.com
  48 units   *Very Expensive*
One of the world's unabashedly best coastal panoramas is
the highlight of this resort hotel and time-share high above
the north end of the Big Sur coast. Lush grounds accented
by Monterey pines sequester a large pool, three whirlpools,
exercise room, complimentary bicycles, and a resort store. The
key attribute of the site is the acclaimed ocean-view restaurant
(see listing) with a new (in 2016) view dining deck and a plush
firelit lounge with live entertainment on weekends. Each
spacious unit offers beautiful contemporary furnishings and
a private deck.
  "Townhouse Spa Suites" (7 of these)—wood-burning
    fireplace, kitchenette, large private epic
    ocean-view balcony, and a raised
    in-bedroom two-person whirlpool.
★ **The Inn at Spanish Bay**   *(831)574-5605   (800)877-0597*
  6 mi. N at 2700 Seventeen-Mile Dr. - Pebble Beach 93953
  pebblebeach.com
  269 units   *Very Expensive*
Perched amid tall Monterey pines and sand dunes on a rise
above the ocean, the three-story complex includes a championship 18-hole golf course with a stellar ocean view (see listing),
putting green, eight tennis courts (including two night-lighted),
rental bicycles, a fitness club, restaurants (see listing); plus a
beach, large pool, whirlpool, saunas, steam rooms, fitness facilities, and miles of scenic trails. Each spacious unit (ranging from
a hotel room to two-bedroom suite) is luxuriously furnished
and has a gas fireplace, private patio or balcony, and honor bar
(refrigerator by request only). Most have a coast or forest view.
  "Ocean Executive Suite"—in-bath whirlpool,
    outstanding ocean view.

★ **La Playa Carmel**   *(831)293-6100   (800)582-8900*
 downtown at Camino Real & 8th Av. (Box 900) - 93921
 laplayahotel.com
 75 units   *Very Expensive*
La Playa Carmel is the village's Grande Dame hideaway. The
four-story landmark with its distinctive Mediterranean style
was built in 1905 and finished in 1907 just beyond the edge of
downtown near the beach. It is now surrounded by impeccably
landscaped grounds with a courtyard pool. Buffet brunch and
wine reception are complimentary. A refined lounge adjoins.
Each room is beautifully furnished and has an honor bar. Some
on the top floor have an ocean view.

 L'Auberge Carmel   *(831)624-8578*
 downtown at Monte Verde St. at 7th Av. - 93921
 laubergecarmel.com
 20 units   *Very Expensive*
A historic downtown building now serves as a small luxury hotel.
The primary feature is **Aubergine**, an intimate restaurant
serving remarkably expensive gourmet dinners. The restaurant's signature breakfast is complimentary. Some beautifully
furnished rooms have a partial ocean view.

 Lobos Lodge   *(831)624-3874*
 downtown at Ocean Av. & Monte Verde St. (Box L1) - 93921
 loboslodge.com
 30 units   *Expensive*
Several buildings comprise this small modern motor inn amid
colorful gardens on the main street a few blocks up from the
beach. A complimentary Continental breakfast is served to
your room and there are afternoon cookies. Each spacious,
beautifully furnished room has a gas fireplace, refrigerator,
and a large private deck. Some have an ocean view.

★ **The Lodge at Pebble Beach**   *(831)624-3811   (800)877-0597*
 3 mi. NW at 1700 17-Mile Dr. (Box 567) - Pebble Beach 93953
 pebblebeach.com
 161 units   *Very Expensive*
The world famous Lodge at Pebble Beach has an incomparable
oceanfront location and a wealth of resort amenities. In addition
to the beach, there is a pool, whirlpool and sauna; legendary
18-hole golf course (see listing); (fee) access to an expansive

state-of-the-art tennis complex; complete spa and relaxation facility (see listing); fitness center; horseback riding (see listing) and bicycle rentals; nature trails; plus restaurants (see listing). Each spacious room is luxuriously furnished and many have a private balcony and/or patio and wood-burning fireplace; some also have a superb ocean view. Some rooms (not overlooking the ocean) have a jetted tub on the patio.

★ **Mission Ranch**   *(831)624-6436   (800)538-8221*
   1 mi. S at 26270 Dolores St. - 93923
   missionranchcarmel.com
   31 units   *Moderate–Very Expensive*
Mission Ranch is Carmel's great in-town resort. A historic 1850s farmhouse is the heart of a collection of charming cottages and lodge buildings on flowery grounds. Beyond, a meadow extends to the gorgeous Pacific coastline at the mouth of Carmel River. An advantage of staying on-site is that it is an easy stroll via a ranch path past sheep grazing in a picturesque pasture to the fine-sand beach at Carmel River State Beach. Continental breakfast is complimentary. Amenities include six championship tennis courts, an exercise room, piano bar, and restaurant with priority seating to Ranch guests (see listing). Each unit is beautifully furnished. Almost all have a refrigerator. Most have a fireplace and a large in-bath whirlpool tub. Many have an ocean view.

"Meadowview triplex" (9 of these)—gas fireplace, in-bath two-person whirlpool tub, private porch with distant pastoral ocean view.

★ **Pine Inn**   *(831)624-3851   (800)228-3851*
   downtown on Ocean bet Lincoln/Monte Verde (Box 250) - 93921
   pine-inn.com
   49 units   *Moderate–Very Expensive*
Carmel's main street landmark is a three-story inn (circa 1889) surrounded by gardens. Plush Victorian furnishings distinguish common areas. There is a link in a chain of upscale Italian restaurants with a still-popular lounge. Breakfast is complimentary during the week. Rooms and suites are well furnished. Some units do have an in-bath whirlpool tub and refrigerator.

#64, #26, #27—refrigerator, some ocean surf view.

Quail Lodge & Golf Club   *(831)624-2888*   *(888)828-8787*
5 mi. SE at 8205 Valley Greens Dr. - 93923
quaillodge.com
93 units   *Very Expensive*
Manicured grounds provide a serene setting for an 18-hole
golf course, golf shop, tennis courts, and a fitness center,
hiking trails, putting green, resort shop and **Edgar's** (L–D—
Expensive) offering contemporary California dishes in a dining
room by a scenic pond. Continental breakfast is complimentary.
Each well-furnished unit has a refrigerator and a private deck
overlooking the small lake, golf course or gardens.

★ **Svendsgaard's Inn**   *(831)624-1511*
downtown at 4th Av. & San Carlos St. (Box 101) - 93921
innsbythesea.com
33 units   *Moderate–Expensive*
This long-established one- and two-level complex has been
meticulously improved and upgraded through the years. It
now features delightful landscaped gardens around a huge
yucca plant. Amenities include a large kidney-shaped pool in
a garden court, complimentary Continental breakfast to the
room, and afternoon cookies. Each unit is beautifully furnished
and has a refrigerator. Many have a gas fireplace.

  #5, #9, #12, #25—raised large two-person whirlpool
            with a window view, microwave, gas fireplace.

★ **Tally Ho Inn**   *(831)624-2232*   *(800)652-2632*
downtown on Monte Verde St. at 5th Av. (Box 3726) - 93921
tallyho-inn.com
12 units   *Expensive–Very Expensive*
This historic complex a downhill stroll from Carmel's sugar-
sand beach was originally the home of a famous American
cartoonist. (Does anyone remember "a tip of the Hatlohat"?)
Over many years it has evolved into an inn full of nostalgic
Carmel-appropriate artifacts and includes rooms that have
ocean views. Continental breakfast and brandy in the afternoon
are complimentary. Some beautifully furnished rooms have a
refrigerator and a private balcony.

  #108—large private ocean-view deck, raised
            gas fireplace, one-person whirlpool.
  "Superior King Suite" (5 of these)—two-person
            whirlpool, raised gas fireplace.

★ **Tickle Pink Inn at Carmel Highlands** *(831)624-1244*
   6 mi. S (on Highway 1) at 155 Highland Dr. - 93923
   ticklepinkinn.com   (800)635-4774
   34 units   *Very Expensive*
For more than half a century, Tickle Pink has been one of the most desirable destination lodgings on the California coast. The property is still owned by the same family and both the luxuriant semitropical and Northwestern vegetation and rooms have been meticulously enhanced and upgraded through time. Complimentary amenities include a bottle of champagne on arrival; evening wine and cheese reception; deluxe Continental breakfast including eggs, a meat dish and fresh baked pastries; plus enjoyment of a large whirlpool next to a brook waterfall with a view of surf crashing against headlands far below. All beautifully furnished rooms have a private view balcony, many with an awesome ocean overlook and a refrigerator.
   #30–#35 ("deluxe suites")—spacious,
            luxuriously furnished, microwave,
            in-room two-person whirlpool,
            Duraflame fireplace, large private
            balcony with remarkable view.

★ **Tradewinds Carmel** *(831)624-2776*
   downtown on Mission St. at 3rd Av. (Box 3403) - 93921
   tradewindscarmel.com
   28 units   *Expensive–Very Expensive*
High on a rise in the northeastern corner of the village, Tradewinds has become one of the most handsome resort-motel-style lodgings on the Peninsula. Spectacular little gardens reflect a feng shui influence apparent in several tucked-away locations on the multilevel property. A Zen waterfall and sculptures complete the meticulous, luxuriant gardens. An elaborate Continental breakfast is complimentary. Each unit is beautifully furnished including a refrigerator; most have a raised gas fireplace and many have a jetted whirlpool tub.
   #19 ("Architectural Digest Room")—
            raised gas fireplace, jetted two-
            person bathtub, large private
            balcony with an expansive view
            beyond town to the ocean.

Carmel

Vagabond's House Inn   *(831)624-7738   (800)262-1262*
downtown at Dolores St. & 4th Av. (Box 2747) - 93921
vagabondshouseinn.com
13 units   *Expensive–Very Expensive*
The Vagabond's House through many years has been refurbished and upgraded while keeping the quaint English Tudor style. Lush landscaping contributes to the appeal of the stone, brick and half-timbered nostalgic architecture. Continental breakfast is brought to the room and afternoon wine and appetizers are also complimentary. There is an on-site spa studio. Each room is well furnished including a refrigerator and microwave, and many have a gas fireplace.

Wayside Inn   *(831)624-5336   (800)832-3224*
downtown at Mission St. & 7th Av. (Box 101) - 93921
innsbythesea.com
22 units   *Expensive–Very Expensive*
Comfortably nostalgic decor contributes to the warm appeal of this contemporary motel in the pines. Expanded Continental breakfast brought to the room and cookies and coffee in the afternoon are complimentary. Each beautifully furnished room has a refrigerator. Some have a kitchen, gas fireplace, or in-bath whirlpool tub.
        #21,#23—private deck, in-room two-
                person whirlpool, gas fireplace.

BASIC INFORMATION

Elevation: 200 feet   Population (2010):   3,730
Location: 125 miles South of San Francisco
Nearest airport with commercial flights: Monterey - 7 miles
Carmel Visitor Center   (831)624-2522   (800)550-4333
   downtown on San Carlos St. between 5th & 6th Avs.
   (Box 4444) - 93921
carmelchamber.org

43

Monterey, California

HISTORY & DESCRIPTION

Monterey is a treasury of superlative history and geography. It is located by Monterey Bay in one of America's most picturesque natural amphitheaters. Its seaport has played a major role in the development of the West Coast for well over two centuries. In 1602, Sebastian Vizcaino became the first white man to set foot in the area. He dubbed it Monterey after the count who was viceroy of New Spain. The idyllic site became the first permanent settlement in California in 1770 when Gaspar de Portola established the first of Spain's four presidios and Father Junipero Serra dedicated the second mission in Alta California. (He relocated it to the present site near the Carmel River a year later.) Monterey was a regional capital for Spain until 1822, and for Mexico until 1846 when the United States annexed California. After California became a state in 1850, the town became a whaling, fishing and canning center. It wasn't until after World War II that its destiny as one of the West's most playful towns was fulfilled.

Today, Cannery Row and Fisherman's Wharf are ingenious, fun-loving transformations from an earlier hard-working era. Nowhere is this more apparent than in the superstar of Cannery Row—the Monterey Bay Aquarium. From outside, it looks like the sardine cannery it once was. Inside, the smell, noise, and toilers are gone, replaced by some of the finest maritime exhibits anywhere. Downtown, a collection of historic landmarks blends with urbane shops and galleries. Gourmet and seaside restaurants are plentiful. Nightlife is exuberant. Recreation on-shore and off-shore is booming and remarkably diverse, thanks to new developments in adventure-oriented equipment and year-round desirable climate. Accommodations range from simply clean and comfortable to notably luxurious—complete with awe-inspiring oceanfront views.

WEATHER

Monterey is located along Monterey Bay in the northeastern third of the Monterey Peninsula. Sheltered from direct exposure to the Pacific Ocean by high hills of the natural amphitheater to the west and south, Monterey shares with Carmel and Pacific Grove (the only two other incorporated communities on the Peninsula) status as one of America's half dozen most desirable "great towns" for climates ideal for comfortably enjoying outdoor recreation year-round. Even in winter, days and evenings are cool but usually frost-free so colorful flowers accent lush green landscapes throughout the season. Occasional Pacific rainstorms during the season contribute well over half of the average annual precipation. Spring marks the beginning of consistently mild weather for enjoying almost all outdoor activities, but enjoyment may be marred for some by common sea breezes and coastal fog. Summer is splendid with warm days and cool evenings. Fall is an appealing extension of summer, with an added attraction—the year's highest temperatures normally occur at this time.

WEATHER PROFILE

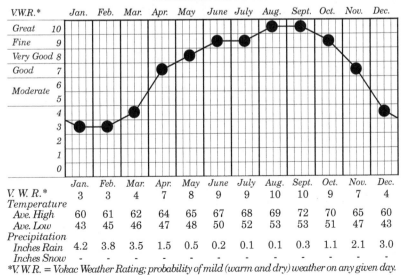

V.W.R.*	Jan.	Feb.	Mar.	Apr.	May	June	July	Aug.	Sept.	Oct.	Nov.	Dec.
V. W. R.*	3	3	4	7	8	9	9	10	10	9	7	4
Temperature												
Ave. High	60	61	62	64	65	67	68	69	72	70	65	60
Ave. Low	43	45	46	47	48	50	52	53	53	51	47	43
Precipitation												
Inches Rain	4.2	3.8	3.5	1.5	0.5	0.2	0.1	0.1	0.3	1.1	2.1	3.0
Inches Snow	-	-	-	-	-	-	-	-	-	-	-	-

*V. W. R. = Vokac Weather Rating; probability of mild (warm and dry) weather on any given day.

ATTRACTIONS

★ *Bicycling*
There are many miles of scenic waterfront trails, bike lanes and off-road tracks in and around Monterey. Most notable are two remarkable routes: the bayside Monterey Peninsula Recreation Trail which extends eighteen miles from Castroville to Pacific Grove, and the renowned Seventeen-Mile Drive between Pacific Grove and Carmel. Assorted bicycles (from single or tandem pedalling or single or tandem electric bikes, and canopy-covered four-wheeled surreys outfitted with two sets of bicycle pedals) can be rented from five convenient locations. Friendly knowledgable staff can also provide any related accessories, maps and information.
Adventures by the Sea *(831)372-1807*
1 mi. NW at 299 Cannery Row
adventuresbythesea.com

★ *Boat Rentals*
Kayaks are especially popular as a way to get an intimate look at sea otters, sea lions, harbor seals and other denizens of the Monterey Bay National Marine Sanctuary (see listing). Water currents are not an issue since this is a relatively sheltered bay of the Pacific Ocean, and conditions are often near perfect in the morning when wind is generally light yet the sun provides enough warmth for comfortable kayaking. All accessorites including proper clothing are available for rent, and knowledgable guides will lead novice tours from the full-service facility below (which is directly across the street from a small sandy beach put-in on Cannery Row). Or, you can opt to go on your own in their one- or two-person kayaks.
Adventures by the Sea *(831)372-1807*
1 mi. NW at 299 Cannery Row
adventuresbythesea.com

Boat Tour
Elkhorn Slough Safari *(831)633-5555*
elkhornslough.com
16 mi. NE at 8022 Moss Landing Rd. - Moss Landing
The key feature of Moss Landing is the Elkhorn Slough. One of the best ways to experience the area is to take a nature boat tour into the numerous watery recesses to check out sea otters,

harbor seals, sea lions and a world-class assortment of birds. The normally calm waters accessed via stable pontoon boats provide ample opportunities for both comfortable viewing and photography for 1½ to 2 hour trips that must be reserved in advance.

★ **Cannery Row**
starts just NW along Cannery Row
canneryrow.com
A few hulking cannery buildings and overpasses across Cannery Row still capture the flavor of the times before sardines vanished from Monterey Bay around 1950. But, the noise and smell described in John Steinbeck's *Cannery Row* are long gone—replaced by a world class aquarium (see listing), and imaginative businesses in ingeniously renovated old buildings and elaborate compatible new structures. The Row is also a staging area for one of America's best beach dives. The continent's deepest near-shore underwater canyon, plus a vast kelp forest and abundant sea life, are nearby offshore from San Carlos Beach (at the beginning of Cannery Row).

El Estero Park Complex   *(831)646-3866*
just E at 777 Pearl St.
monterey.org
This big park next to downtown has walkways, an exereise course, a snack bar, picnic areas, and fishing piers around a picturesque little lake with paddleboat rentals. For family fun, Dennis the Menace Playground is where Hank Ketchum, creator of "Dennis the Menace," helped develop free-form "hands-on" play equipment. Narrow tunnels, balanced roundabouts, swinging bridges, giant slides, and other unusual devices entice children of all ages. Closed Mon. from November to May.

★ **Fisherman's Wharf**
downtown at the N end of Alvarado St.
montereywharf.com
Original commercial fishing activities that operated here since 1845 are long gone. The wharf remains and over-water buildings along it have evolved into a colorful potpourri of shops, restaurants, and open-air fish markets. Visitors are drawn by the bracing nautical atmosphere, marine views, close-up glimpses of harbor seals, sea otters, and aquatic birds.

This is also the Peninsula's major terminus for sportfishing and sightseeing boats.

★ *Fishing Charters*
   downtown on Fisherman's Wharf
Several sportfishing boats leave daily year-round for deep sea fishing. Memorable winter whale watching excursions and narrated sightseeing cruises are also featured. Many operators, located on Fisherman's Wharf, offer these services and all necessary equipment. Chris' is the oldest and largest whale-watching company on Monterey Bay. Their experienced skippers narrate the tours on boats with bathrooms and comfortable seating.

   Chris' Fishing & Whale Watching   *(831)375-5951*
   downtown at 48 Fisherman's Wharf #1
   chrissfishing.com

Food Specialties
   Moss Landing   *(831)633-3038*
   18 mi. N at 7902 Hwy. 1 - Moss Landing
Sprawled along the highway at the turnout to Moss Landing is the Whole Enchilada complex. At the corner is a big atmospheric subtropical Mexican-style restaurant. Next door is a large shop that showcases seasonally fresh produce from this region. The artichoke is king here and can be enjoyed in a number of different treats, fresh or in jars. At the other end is a market that uses fresh local ingredients for deli delights and a wine tasting area adjoins a colorful dining room.

Golf
★   **Del Monte Golf Course**   *(831)373-2700*
   1 mi. SE at 1300 Sylvan Rd.
The oldest course in continuous operation west of the Mississippi has been played for well over a century. A putting green and pro shop, and some food services, are available at the 18-hole regulation course which is a must for golf history buffs.

   Jacks Peak Regional Park   *(831)755-4899*   *(888)588-2267*
   5 mi. SE via Hwy. 68 at 25020 Jacks Peak Park Rd.
   co.monterey.ca.us
Panoramic views of the peninsula and coastline and miles of hiking trails are features of the high preserve of Monterey pine-forested hills south of town. A mile-long nature trail

provides a scenic loop to the 1,068-foot peak. Open 10:00 a.m. until between 5-7 p.m.

★ **Marina State Beach** *(831)649-2836*
  11 mi. N at foot of Reservation Rd. - Marina
  parks.ca.gov
The region's best day-use combination dune-and-beach park features views of Monterey Bay and the city in the distance that are outstanding from the blufftop parking area (with a surprising amount of free parking). There are designated sandy trails down the dunes to a wide expansive beach. Because this is the eastern end of Monterey Bay, the surf is often spectacular as a result of consistent wind blowing off the Pacific Ocean.

★ **Monterey Bay Aquarium** *(831)648-4800*
  1 mi. NW at 886 Cannery Row
  montereybayaquarium.org
One of the world's biggest and best aquariums is in an ingeniously remodeled cannery complex that extends into the ocean at Monterey Bay. Visitors are given a unique and exciting view of native inhabitants of Monterey Bay—sea otters, octopus, salmon, sharks, jellyfish, and hundreds of other species of flora and fauna in an interactive naturalistic setting. A highlight is feeding time in a three-story kelp forest in a towering glass-walled tank. More than one hundred close-up viewing tanks, six giant tanks, and an expanded family-friendly splash zone display near-shore-to-outer-bay environs and creatures ranging from starfish to vast schools of sardines (in a truly hypnotic glass-walled circular tank) and giant sea turtles. A deep reef exhibit features giant octopus. Another exhibit, "Wild about Otters," contains many international sea otter species. Special exhibits like "Viva Baja! Life on the Edge" and "Tentacles" are major evolving displays. In **Cindy's Waterfront** (L only—Moderate), contemporary California fare is served by a window wall with binoculars on each table for viewing offshore birds, seals, otters, even dolphin and grey whales. On windy days, storm surf blowing against the reinforced window wall can also be thrilling. You can make a reservation at 648-4870, but window seating is first-come, first-served. There is also a casual self-service cafe with pizzas, beverages, and desserts. Near the entrance is a large excellent gift-and-book shop.

★ **Monterey Bay National Marine Sanctuary** *(831)647-4201*
  just N
  montereybay.noaa.gov
The nation's largest marine preserve covers 4,601 nautical miles of ocean extending an average of thirty miles from shore. It includes Monterey Canyon. As deep as the Grand Canyon, it is one of the deepest submarine canyons next to America's west coast. The Monterey Peninsula and Big Sur coasts provide exceptional gateways to offshore areas teeming with colorful vegetation, fish, crustaceans and marine mammals.

★ **Monterey Sports Center** *(831)646-3730*
  downtown at 301 E. Franklin St.
  monterey.org/sportscenter
Day use passes are available to visitors for this enormous contemporary sports complex which includes two indoor pools with many separated 25-yard-long lap lanes. A winding (112 feet) waterslide is open during limited swim times geared for children. Men's and women's saunas, showers, lockers, and towel rentals are available. Exercise equipment of all kinds is available in abundance. There is also a comfortable little cafe where you can relax and enjoy simple casual fare.

★ **Monterey State Historical Park** *(831)649-7118*
  downtown at 20 Custom House Plaza
  parks.ca.gov
California's European colonial history began here. Well over two centuries of impressive history and architectural heritage in California's oldest town are carefully preserved near Fisherman's Wharf, and in numerous downtown buildings. **Pacific House** is a museum with interactive pre-statehood exhibits. The **Custom House** is the oldest government building in California. **Larkin House** (1834), combining Spanish-Colonial and New England architectural features, became a prototype copied throughout California. Robert Lewis Stevenson boarded and wrote in the **Stevenson House** in 1879. **Colton Hall** (1848), the first American public building in California, was where the state's first constitution was written in 1849. **Cooper-Molera Adobe** includes gardens, barns and farm animals, and a visitor center on expansive grounds. **Royal Presidio Chapel** (the state's oldest church in continuous use) has served since 1795.

50

★ **National Steinbeck Center**   *(831)775-4721*
17 mi. NE at One Main St. - Salinas
steinbeck.org
The National Steinbeck Center is a large state-of-the-art museum and archive dedicated to one of America's most renowned authors. The center, at the head of main street in downtown Salinas (Steinbeck's birthplace), presents a wealth of interactive multi-sensory exhibits. Seven themed theaters showcase his life and work featuring clips from *Cannery Row*, *East of Eden*, and other movies from his books. The original camper that was home to the author and his poodle while they researched *Travels With Charley* is a highlight. An orientation theater shows a brief biographical film of Steinbeck's life, while a changing gallery displays a variety of related art exhibits. Other features include comprehensive archives and a well-stocked museum store featuring all kinds of Steinbeck memorabilia. The museum is open seven days a week year-round.

Spas

★ **Casa Munras Garden Hotel & Spa**   *(831)372-1829*
just S at 700 Munras Av.
hotelcasamunras.com/day-spa
The Spa at Casa Munras is one of the best on the Monterey Peninsula. Here is a complete resort facility that captures the spirit of Monterey in both treatments offered and the facility's decor. Guests can enjoy relaxation areas, a waterfall whirlpool, a lush garden grotto with a large kidney-shaped swimming pool, exercise room, and a wealth of massage treatments attuned to the spirit of this unique area. Talented staff provide everything from a variety of traditional hour or longer massages to packages. One that stands out is for romantically inclined couples interested in sharing a massage followed by champagne and fresh fruit in an adjoining private, candle-lighted large hot tub.

★ **Monterey Plaza Hotel & Spa**   *(831)920-6710*
1 mi. NW at 400 Cannery Row
montereyplazahotel.com
Vista Blue is the Peninsula's finest spa right by the ocean. The tranquil end of the top floor of the Monterey Plaza Hotel was designed from the beginning to provide a serene setting

for rejuvenating the body and senses. Facilities for spa guests age 13 and up include a full range of massage treatments in the comfort of individual rooms or a special couples'spa room. Body treatments utilize components like rosemary sea salt and rituals like soaks with an abundance of bubbles. Skin care for men and women is also taken seriously along with oxygen infusion where "cooling calming oxygen under light pressure is applied directly to the skin surface." Both men's and women's facilities include a complete range of changing areas, shower, sauna and relaxation/waiting rooms. To top it all off (literally) there is an outdoor deck on the roof with two whirlpools overlooking the ocean almost directly below, together with lounging facilities to catch sun rays or to enjoy a fire in the fireplace. Both men and women can take advantage of advanced high-tech fitness equipment. Food service from the hotel is available and there is a well-stocked gift shop with many samples of first-rate body moisturizers. All facilities are available to hotel guests as well.

Theater

Bruce Ariss Wharf Theater   *(831)649-2332*
downtown at 1 Fisherman's Wharf
montereywharf.com
For more than forty years, Wharf Theater has been pleasing theater-goers at this location with exuberant performances of musicals and dramas in an intimate playhouse on the Wharf.

★ ***Wineries***   *(831)375-9400*
montereywines.org   riverroadwinetrail.com
Within an hour's drive of Monterey are ten wineries with tasting facilities located along the **River Road Wine Trail** and on the Santa Lucia Highlands bench above the Salinas River Valley. Limited productions of premium varietals, warm hospitality and opportunities to meet and sample with actual winemakers have made River Road a major wine touring destination. Meanwhile, back in Monterey, there are four notable tasting rooms:

A Taste of Monterey   *(831)646-5446*
1 mi. NW at 700 Cannery Row (upstairs)
atasteofmonterey.com
Taste selections from more than ninety Monterey County wineries for a (refundable) fee and purchase from seventy-plus regional wines while watching ocean swells which seem to

roll under your waterfront table. It can be accompanied by a wealth of tapas-style contemporary dishes. Tour wineries via their film. The shop displays and sells a large selection of wine and related accessories and gourmet foods. Open daily 11–6.

Bargetto Winery Tasting Room   *(831)373-4053*
1 mi. NW at 700-G Cannery Row   (800)422-7438
bargetto.com
A wide selection of Bargetto wines is available for tasting. There are a couple of standouts as the chardonnay and pinot noir have become award winners. Open daily 11–6:30.

Carmel Ridge Winery Tasting Room   *(831)324-0035*
1 mi. NW at 700-C Cannery Row
carmelridge.com
Carmel Ridge Winery does nice work with chardonnay and sauvignon blanc and has a deservedly award-winning pinot noir reserve. Tasting flights are available and seasonal wood platters feature artisan cheeses, cured meats, olives and other regional provisions. You can also purchase wines by the glass. Open 11–9 or later.

Roadhouse Wine Bar   *(831)372-1909*
4 mi. SE at 2999 Monterey/Salinas Hwy. 68
pumaroad.com
An atmospheric old limestone building has been contemporized. Beyond some handsome old rock walls, a spiffy tasting area features wood-trim picture windows and mirrors overlooking luxuriant tree-shaded hills and gardens. Enjoy Tarpy's gourmet appetizers (like ale-washed giant Bavarian pretzel with sea salt) that you can order here while enjoying both Puma Road and **Pessagno** estate bottling. **Puma Road** produces consistent quality cabernets, pinots and chardonnays. Open noon–7.

RESTAURANTS

★ **Alvarado Street Brewery & Grill** *(831)655-2337*
downtown at 426 Alvarado St.
alvaradostreetbrewery.com
L–D. Moderate
Traditional and updated California pub grub includes menu surprises like Manhattan clam chowder, truffle crawfish, mac 'n cheese, Vietnamese lamb burger, chicken pot pie, and fried Brussels sprouts. The snazzy post-modern bar and dining hall overlook views of brew kettles behind the backbar, a semi-expo kitchen, and lots of giant-size colorful beer ad posters. A large outdoor wood-trim dining area is out back.

The Breakfast Club *(831)394-3238*
3 mi. E at 1130 Fremont Blvd. - Seaside
bclubcafe.com
B–L–D. Moderate
The Breakfast Club, aptly named, is a pleasant surprise in an unassuming little shopping center tucked away in Seaside. An ambitious menu offers a full range of morning dishes. Consider crabcake benedict or chile verde omelet with avocado and sour cream, or cinnamon roll pancakes, bananas foster french toast, or homemade corned beef hash. Later in the day, a wide range of California comfort foods is offered for lunch and dinner. Wooden tables and chairs fill the large cheerful coffee shop and small adjoining lounge.

Cafe Fina *(831)372-5200*
downtown at 47 Fisherman's Wharf
cafefina.com
L–D. Expensive
A smooth blend of classic Italian and innovative California cuisine is showcased in fresh seafood like cioppino or grilled sand dabs, wood-fired small pizzas, and housemade desserts. Harbor-view tables upstairs are notable.

Cannery Row Brewing Company *(831)643-2722*
1 mi. NW at 95 Prescott Av.
canneryrowbrewingcompany.com
L–D. Moderate
Traditional pub grub includes everything from Parmesan pretzels and Guinness-battered corn dogs through pulled pork

sandwich; fisherman's stew; or hickory-smoked pork chops; plus monkey bread donuts for dessert. Half a dozen wheat beers and two dozen pale ales are among 74 tap beers. A historic building has been transformed to include several atmospheric pub areas and a nifty three-fire-ring deck overlooking part of the heart of Cannery Row.

★ **Casa Munras Garden Hotel & Spa**   *(831)375-0176*
   just S at 700 Munras Av.
   hotelcasamunras.com/esteban-restaurant
   B–D.   *Expensive*
Estéban is all about a wide range of skillfully prepared Mediterranean tapas-style specialties. Possibilities range from distinctive creative appetizers to traditional Spanish classic paellas or Monterey Bay seafood stew, or first-rate Western-style Hanger steak. Wrap up with homemade desserts like beignet-style churros and sweet-and-savory treats like strawberry-goat cheese empanadas. The wood-trim dining room has a warm inviting appeal enhanced by a large patio with dramatic freestanding fireplaces.

★ **Chart House**   *(831)372-3362*
   1 mi. NW at 444 Cannery Row
   chart-house.com
   D only.   *Expensive*
Contemporary California-style seafoods, steaks, and vegies like herb-steamed artichoke are served in the Peninsula's large representative of the upscale dinner house. But the food must compete for each diner's attention with spectacular Monterey Bay views from the rocky permanent perch by the waterfront. Playful sea otters and other marine animals are often seen from waterfront tables set amid comfortably retro-rustic decor.

Crown & Anchor   *(831)649-6496*
   downtown at 150 W. Franklin St.
   crownandanchor.net
   L–D.   *Moderate*
An authentic Brit bill of fare like corned beef and cabbage, steak-and-mushroom pie, and fish and chips is served in a bar and dining areas awash in Britannia objects of art and decor touches. The heated little dining patio out back is another popular hangout.

★ **Crystal Fish** *(831)649-3474*
1 mi. NW at 514 Lighthouse Av.
crystalfishmonterey.com
L–D. No L Sat. & Sun. *Moderate*
Monterey's best Japanese restaurant is this simply comfortable dining room and sushi bar. They do it all, from tempting sushi specialties at the expo prep counter to classic and creative dishes skillfully prepared as teriyaki, tempura and other styles of cooked entrees. For lunch, the two- or three-specialty bento boxes are an outstanding treat as well. Save room for distinctive desserts like tasty tempura banana with green tea ice cream, or mango pudding.

★ **Domenico's on the Wharf** *(831)372-3655*
downtown at 50 Fisherman's Wharf
domenicosmonterey.com
L–D. *Expensive*
It's said that success is in attention to detail. Here, that axiom is delightfully brought off in the best restaurant on Fisherman's Wharf. For more than a third of a century, the owner has paid meticulous attention to his cuisine and the atmosphere of his extraordinary restaurant where a window wall and mirrors give every patron a splendid view of the marina and Monterey Pine-shrouded mountains behind it. Classic and innovative California cuisine is consistently delicious. Consider Monterey Bay sardines marinated and grilled Sicilian style, or Point Reyes blue cheese iceberg wedge, and for an entree, whole Dungeness crab prepared five ways, or cedar-planked wild salmon. Luscious housemade desserts include the family's outstanding traditional tiramisu. Many dining tables outfitted with full linen, candles and flowers overlook boats in the adjoining inner harbor.

The Fish Hopper *(831)372-8543*
1 mi. NW at 700 Cannery Row
fishhopper.com
L–D. *Expensive*
One of the largest restaurants on the Peninsula is the original Fish Hopper. Seafood is emphasized on a contemporary American menu, but the reason to be here is the view. Some tables are actually in an alcove built over the Pacific Ocean, and there is a sunny heated bay-view deck.

Fishwife   *(831)394-2027*
3 mi. E at 789 Trinity Av. - Seaside
fishwife.com
L–D. Closed Sun.   *Moderate*
Traditional Mexican and American seafood specialties include
grilled king salmon with habanero butter sauce; sautéed sole
Doré; or grilled sand dabs. The simply furnished little dining
room is supplemented by umbrella-shaded sidewalk dining.

Gianni's Pizza   *(831)649-1500*
1 mi. NW at 725 Lighthouse Av.
mygiannis.com
L–D. No L Mon.–Thurs.   *Moderate*
Since 1974, this family-owned restaurant has featured all kinds
of thick-crust pizza with designer or you-select toppings, plus
assorted calzones. Tempting desserts—pies and gelatos—are
also displayed and served in big warm dining rooms.

Grandma's Kitchen   *(831)375-3033*
2 mi. E at 2310 Fremont St.
B–L–D.   *Moderate*
Grandma's all-American coffee shop is delightfully awash in
nostalgia. Their flower garden showcases Pride of Madeira
(which in springtime has hundreds of foot-long purple flower
brachts). Inside, chrome-trim overstuffed formica chairs and
booths and nifty bric-a-brac on the walls complete the comfortable 1950s feel. Traditional American comfort foods in generous
portions range from various omelets to waffles or distinctive
pancakes with some unusual specialties like pine nut and
banana, or housemade old-timey biscuits with a choice of two
gravies.

★ **Hula's**   *(831)655-4852*
1 mi. NW at 622 Lighthouse Av.
hulastiki.com
L–D. No L Sun. & Mon.   *Moderate*
Monterey's nod to Hawaii is a lively Tiki-style bar and raised
dining room with tasty Island classics like potstickers, a luau
pork plate, or macadamia nut or coconut-encrusted fish flown
in from Hawaii. Generous portions served amid rattan, bamboo,
surfboards and related wall art contribute to the pleasing
casual "Islands" spirit.

Intercontinental The Clement Monterey   *(831)375-4800*
1 mi. NW at 750 Cannery Row
ictheclementmonterey.com/dining.aspx
B–L–D.   *Very Expensive*
In the hotel's **C Restaurant & Bar**, contemporary California cuisine is featured in dishes ranging from Monterey Bay calamari to entrees like wild sea bass or New York steak. Sustainable seasonal products, local where possible, contribute to the appeal. So does the partially blocked window wall view of the bay beyond a walkway. The expansive dining room provides a choice of tables and chairs or padded banquettes. A heated deck adjoins which shares the view.

★ **Lalla Oceanside Grill**   *(831)324-0891*
1 mi. NW at 654 Cannery Row
lallamonterey.com
L–D.   *Moderate*
Contemporary California dishes include an appropriate emphasis on fish and crustaceans backed by fresh seasonal fruits and vegetables of the region. Specialty drinks in adventurous combinations like green ice tea with melon and pomegranate or peach lemonade complement skillfully prepared meals and desserts. The dining room is as delightful as the cuisine thanks to a fifty-foot-long window wall adjoining the bay and Pacific Ocean. The spiffy comfort of raised banquettes or padded chairs at tables by the windows, and post-modern touches like neo-crystal lamps, fresh flowers and candles contribute to au courant charm. There is also a covered sidewalk patio and a downstairs bar.

★ **Lallapalooza**   *(831)645-9036*
downtown at 474 Alvarado St.
lallamonterey.com
D only.   *Expensive*
An expo kitchen serves a fine range of all-American updates like baseball-cut prime sirloin, cedar-planked salmon, or seafood chowder. A dessert highlight is their chocolate banana cream pie, a luscious post-modern update on an American classic. A snazzy wood-trim dining room has banquettes and hardwood tables and chairs backed by big colorful wall hangings, a see-through wine cellar, and a sleek lounge.

★ **Loulou's Griddle in the Middle**   *(831)372-0568*
just E on Municipal Wharf #2
loulousgriddle.com
B–L. Closed Tues.   *Moderate*
Loulou's lively little cafe on the bay is a locals' favorite. Nifty
nautical surroundings contribute to the appeal, too, since it's
perched on the edge of the second wharf with a view of historic
Fisherman's Wharf and downtown beyond boats in the marina.
Fine specialties include tender pancakes filled with bananas
or strawberries, or a sizable seafood omelet.
Massaro & Santos   *(831)649-6700*
just N at 32 Cannery Row, Suite H-1
massaroandsantos.com
L–D.   *Expensive*
Massaro & Santos is a seafood house popular with locals. From
silky Boston clam chowder to delicate local sand dabs or crab
ravioli, each dish is fresh and flavorful. Most glass-topped tables
around three sides of the upstairs dining room have a pleasing
view of Monterey's marine scene. An adjoining heated dining
porch shares the view.
★ **Monterey Plaza Hotel & Spa**   *(831)920-6710*
1 mi. NW at 400 Cannery Row
montereyplazahotel.com/dining
B–L–D.   *Expensive*
In **Schooners Coastal Kitchen & Bar**, fresh seafood, prime
meats and top-quality seasonal produce are skillfully transformed into regional dishes like scaloppine of Monterey red
abalone, Central Coast artichoke chowder, or fisherman's
cioppino. The casually elegant wood-trimmed dining room
offers panoramic picture-window views of Monterey Bay and
the Pacific Ocean from a location almost over the water. An
expansive umbrella-shaded deck, deservedly popular on pleasant
days, shares the comfortably close waterside setting.
★ **Monterey's Fish House**   *(831)373-4647*
2 mi. E at 2114 Del Monte Av.
L–D. No L Sat. & Sun.   *Moderate*
One of the Peninsula's best seafood specialty houses is in
an unassuming freestanding dining room and lounge by the
highway. The kitchen has great skill in contemporary treatments

of generous portions of assorted fresh fish and shellfish. Every item from the breads through desserts (including housemade carrot cake and cannoli) is delicious. Examples of outstanding specialties include oak-grilled oysters, or steamed artichokes, grilled sole Doré, traditional Italian cioppino, and French Bouillabaisse. Glass-topped tables set with flowers and linen napkins outfit two dining rooms, and there is a similarly casual bar.

Montrio Bistro   *(831)648-8880*
downtown at 414 Calle Principal
montrio.com
D only.   *Expensive*
A grazing menu of European-inspired post-modern dishes (like double lamb chops with minted spinach hummus or scallop with avocado-jalapeno panna cotta) has made this restaurant an au courant favorite. Stylish dining rooms have been fashioned within a historic Monterey firehouse along with a whimsical bar.

Old Fisherman's Grotto   *(831)375-4604*
downtown at 39 Fisherman's Wharf
oldfishermansgrotto.com
L–D.   *Expensive*
For more than half a century, Old Fisherman's Grotto has been serving visitors, especially families, with all sorts of traditional seafoods (of the region and beyond) plus steaks, poultry and pastas. Casual dining room booths include many window tables with bayfront views.

★ **Paris Bakery**   *(831)646-1620*
downtown at 271 Bonifacio Place
parisbakery.us
B–L.   *Moderate*
Sequestered on a side street near the heart of Monterey is one of the best and most comprehensive bakeries in California. Bear claws, cinnamon rolls, scones, and many other morning delights are consistently excellent, while croissants with ham and cheese or croque monsieur make flavorful lunches. Assorted breads including the regional specialty, sourdough, and luscious desserts displayed in many cases are backed by nearly a dozen tables where tantalizing baked goods can be viewed and enjoyed with assorted coffees or to go.

Parker-Lusseau
 downtown at 731 Munras Av. *(831)643-0300*
 downtown at 539 Hartnell St. *(831)641-9188*
 parker-lusseaupastries.com
 B–L. *Moderate*
Careful selection from among the dozen-or-so pastries can result in a memorable morning delight. Selected ciabatta and other breads are made in the downstairs bakery that has a couple of tables and casual outdoor seating. The patisserie (on Hartnell) is tiny, charming, and open every day for takeout. Munras Av. location is closed Sun.-Tues.

Phil's Fish Market & Eatery *(831)633-2152*
 16 mi. NE at 7600 Sandholdt Rd., on the island - Moss Landing
 philsfishmarket.com
 L–D. *Moderate*
At Phil's cavernous funky fish market/deli/restaurant where you wait in line to order, you can get your fill of regional fresh seafood charbroiled, breaded, grilled, fried or in pastas and sandwiches. A big bowl of acclaimed cioppino brings it all together in a memorable way. You can also get artichokes seven different ways including steamed, stuffed, french-fried or Sicilian style. There is plenty of really casual indoor and outdoor seating including picnic tables extending almost to a sandy shore overlooking surf, or you can get it to go.

Portola Hotel & Spa *(831)649-7874*
 downtown at 2 Portola Plaza
 portolahotel.com/jacks-restaurant-lounge
 B–L–D. *Expensive*
Jacks Restaurant offers contemporary California fare in bistro selections like Monterey Bay sand dabs, lobster cioppino or 14-ounce Angus ribeye steak. The very large dining rooms feature a choice of comfortable armchairs or banquettes backed by stylish wood-trim walls with Monterey-related art. **Jacks Lounge** is a plush piano firelit getaway.

Red's Donuts *(831)372-9761*
 downtown at 533 Alvarado St.
 redsdonuts.com
 B–L. *Low*
Since 1950, Red's has been a key source for handmade sweet treats.

Restaurant 1833   *(831)643-1833*
downtown at 500 Hartnell St.
restaurant1833.com
D only.   *Expensive*
One of Monterey's most historic homes now serves as a source
for contemporary eclectic cuisine like sunchokes, sweetbreads,
and lamb sausage on a fusion menu. Beyond a nostalgic firelit
lounge outfitted with Victorian overstuffed furniture is a
casually elegant dining room with a garden view.

Rosine's Restaurant   *(831)375-6400*
downtown at 434 Alvarado St.
rosinesmonterey.com
B–L–D.   *Moderate*
For more than a third of a century, Rosine's has been a destination for breakfast, American comfort foods, and stellar desserts.
Several display cases are full of cakes and pies. The size and
variety are remarkable, and quality is good in humongous treats
like the six-inch-tall carrot cake. A choice of booths or padded
chairs contributes to the popularity of the big casual dining room.

★ **Sardine Factory**   *(831)373-3775*
1 mi. NW at 701 Wave St.
sardinefactory.com
D only.   *Very Expensive*
Fresh local seafood and gracious cosmopolitan atmosphere have
distinguished the Peninsula's longest-established gourmet dinner
house for nearly fifty years. Remarkably, the stellar quality of
the cuisine has endured, and the gifted chefs continue to delight
patrons with creative treatments of the freshest possible ingredients. Traditional and contemporary specialties include peerless
abalone bisque, pan-seared local sand dabs, and lobster ravioli.
Locally sourced top-quality Salinas Valley iceberg lettuce stars in
a salad with memorable pecan-smoked bacon, artichoke hearts,
tomato and blue cheese dressing. Beef and lamb selections are
also expertly prepared. Save room for a selection from a long list
of luscious desserts like the Italian trio of cannoli, tiramisu and
spumoni. The capacious restaurant offers a variety of elegant
dining venues, including a gilt and rococo firelit Victorian room.
The grand glass-domed conservatory is the perfect setting for
Monterey's premier fine dining experience.

Sea Harvest Fish Market & Restaurant   *(831)646-0547*
1 mi. NW at 598 Foam St.
seaharvestfish.com
L–D.   *Moderate*
Beyond several display cases full of seasonal fresh local fish
and shellfish is a simply outfitted dining area with a dozen
tables. You can enjoy all styles of seafood cocktails, chowders,
sandwiches and pastas, plus fried or grilled entrees, here or
to go.
Tarpy's Roadhouse   *(831)647-1444*
5 mi. SE at 2999 Salinas Hwy. (Hwy. 68)
tarpys.com
L–D. Sun. brunch.   *Expensive*
Zesty contemporary American dishes like crispy kale leaves
or roasted artichoke for starters distinguish a grazing menu
that extends to luscious desserts. Several intimate dining
areas and a lounge are backed by colorful wall art, a notable
clam-shell fireplace, and picture-window views of the lush
adjoining garden court.
Whaling Station Steakhouse   *(831)373-3778*
1 mi. NW at 763 Wave St.
whalingstation.net
D only.   *Expensive*
The waiter displays all of the high-end cuts of beef raw on a
tray to trigger your carnivorous urges. Slow-roasted prime rib
is also a house specialty, and there are seafood alternatives.
The fully linened old-fashioned steakhouse hasn't changed
much in more than forty years.
Zimatlan Bakery & Deli   *(831)869-0464*
3 mi. E at 1291 Fremont Blvd. - Seaside
zimatlanbakery.com
B–L.   *Low*
Zimatlan Bakery & Deli is a fine source for authentic Mexican
pastries and bread products including cookies and cakes of
interior and border Mexico. It's all available to go with traditional light Mexican dishes or to enjoy in the plain little dining
room beyond the display racks.

LODGINGS

Lodgings are abundant and diverse including resorts, waterfront motor inns, and gracious bed-and-breakfasts. Munras Avenue and Fremont Street are the Peninsula's motel rows where in recent years, most bargain motels have been upgraded both in quality and price. June–to–October is the highest season. Rates on weekends, especially Saturday night, are generally significantly higher than during weekdays year-round; and there are essentially no budget lodgings on the Peninsula. During special event weekends (which are frequent), some lodgings that are normally affordable (especially on Fremont Street) charge exorbitant rates. Many lodgings have a two-day or three-day minimum at peak times. For visitors who cannot avoid being there at those popular times but cannot afford the prices, the best bet is the relatively easy drive to Salinas where moderately priced lodgings are usually available.

America's Best Value Presidents Inn   *(831)373-2761*
   just S at 1150 Munras Av. - 93940
   abvi.com
   46 units   *Moderate*
This nicely landscaped two-story motel by the highway has been attractively upgraded in recent times. Amenities include an outdoor pool, whirlpool, and complimentary expanded Continental breakfast. Each well-furnished unit includes a mini-refrigerator and microwave, but no air conditioning. The chain also has a nearby representative in Seaside.

★ **Arbor Inn**   *(831)372-4687*
   just S at 1058 Munras Av. - 93940
   arborinnmonterey.com
   55 units   *Moderate*
Attractively framed in gardens, this contemporary updated and upscaled two-story motel offers a complimentary expanded Continental breakfast with tasty warm biscuits and gravy and waffles. Each well-furnished room includes high-tech lamps with power bases, and has a refrigerator and microwave. Some rooms include a gas fireplace.

Best Western Plus Victorian Inn   *(831)373-8000*
   1 mi. N at 487 Foam St. - 93940   *(800)232-4141*
   victorianinn.com

64

70 units   *Expensive–Very Expensive*

All of Cannery Row is an easy stroll from this contemporary three-story lodging. Features include underground parking, complimentary expanded Continental breakfast and evening wine-and-cheese reception. Each well-furnished room has some combination of raised gas fireplace, private patio, balcony, or window seat, and they all have a refrigerator.

★ **Casa Munras Garden Hotel & Spa**   *(831)375-2411*
just S at 700 Munras Av. - 93940
   163 units   *Expensive–Very Expensive*
hotelcasamunras.com

This is Monterey's classic garden court resort hotel. One of Monterey's oldest genteel motor hotels with an idyllic location adjacent to, but quieter than, downtown has evolved into a large romantic getaway resort. Amenities include dramatic, colorful landscaping throughout; a distinguished Sano spa (see listing); a large grotto garden pool and whirlpool; exercise room; complimentary afternoon cookies; plus **Estéban,** a fine dining room (see listing), and lounge. Rental bicycles are also available. The whole facility was upgraded and contemporized while retaining the Monterey style and charm in 2016. Many of the beautifully furnished rooms feature a raised gas fireplace and some have a refrigerator.

Clarion Hotel Monterey   *(831)373-1337   (800)424-6423*
just S at 1046 Munras Av. - 93940
clarionhotelmonterey.com
   55 units   *Moderate–Expensive*

An attractive large indoor pool is the center of interest, and there is also a whirlpool and sauna in this stylish two-story motel. Continental breakfast is complimentary. Each room is spacious and well furnished including a refrigerator and microwave. Several rooms also have either a whirlpool or a gas fireplace. The "Honeymoon Suite" has both.

Colton Inn   *(831)649-6500   (800)848-7007*
downtown at 707 Pacific St. - 93940
coltoninn.com
   50 units   *Moderate–Expensive*

This modern motel has a convenient downtown location and a sauna. Continental breakfast is complimentary and you can enjoy it on a large deck, plus afternoon cookies and fresh fruit. Each room is well furnished and has a refrigerator and microwave. Some have a Duraflame fireplace, or large whirlpool.

El Castell Motel   *(831)372-8176*
 2 mi. E at 2102 N. Fremont St. - 93940
 elcastellmotel.com
 55 units   *Moderate–Expensive*
This older, simply landscaped long-established predominantly one-story motel features a large indoor pool. The rooms have been modernized and include a refrigerator and microwave.

Embassy Suites Hotel Monterey Bay   *(831)393-1115*
 2 mi. E at 1441 Canyon Del Rey - Seaside 93955   (800)362-2779
 embassymonterey.com
 234 units   *Very Expensive*
A large indoor pool, whirlpool, sauna, fitness center, on-site bicycle rentals, gift shop with a good selection of local books, restaurant and lounge are features of this business-oriented twelve-story hotel. So are the complimentary expanded Continental breakfast and afternoon manager's reception. An ocean beach is only two blocks away. Major renovation begins in fall 2016. Each well-furnished unit has a refrigerator and microwave. Higher rooms have some view of distant surf.

Hilton Garden Inn   *(831)373-6141*
 1 mi. S at 1000 Aquajito Rd. - 93940
 monterey.hgi.com
 204 units   *Expensive–Very Expensive*
Amenities of the three-story conventional complex include a large garden pool and whirlpool, fitness room, and restaurant. Each spacious, well-furnished unit has a private deck, refrigerator and microwave, and some have a garden view.

★ **Hotel Abrego**   *(831)372-7551   (800)982-1986*
 just S at 755 Abrego St. - 93940
 hotelabrego.com
 93 units   *Expensive*
Conveniently located next to downtown, this recently upgraded contemporary three-story motor hotel has a pool, whirlpool, fitness facilities, and bistro. Each room is beautifully furnished and includes a refrigerator. Most have a balcony or patio.
     "Deluxe Rooms"(9 of these)—spacious,
              gas fireplace, private balcony.

Hotel Pacific *(831)373-5700   (800)554-5542*
downtown at 300 Pacific St. - 93940
hotelpacific.com
105 units   *Expensive*
Hotel Pacific is a four-story all-suites hotel. Graceful adobe
buildings are enhanced by intimate garden courtyards with
two whirlpools. A Continental breakfast is complimentary.
Each spacious well-furnished suite has a gas fireplace and a
private patio or terrace.

★ **Hyatt Regency - Monterey** *(831)372-1234*
1 mi. SE at 1 Old Golf Course Rd. - 93940
monterey.hyatt.com
550 units   *Expensive–Very Expensive*
A scenic 18-hole golf course adjoins Monterey's largest lodging,
a well-landscaped four-story resort and conference center which
has just completed a major resort renovation. Amenities include
adjacent golf (see listing for **Del Monte Golf Course**), six
tennis courts, rental bicycles, two pools, two whirlpools, fully
equipped fitness center, full service spa, ping pong, gift shop,
Tusca (B–D—Expensive) restaurant, entertainment lounge,
and sports bar **Knuckles** (D only). Most beautifully furnished
rooms and suites have golf course views and a refrigerator. All
reflect the refined restraint of these green times.

★ **Intercontinental The Clement Monterey** *(831)375-4500*
1 mi. NW at 750 Cannery Row - 93940
ictheclementmonterey.com
208 units   *Very Expensive*
The Peninsula's newest major hotel has a choice location by the
bay on Cannery Row near the Aquarium. Amenities include a
lap pool, whirlpool and fitness center in the spa where a variety
of facials, massage and body treatments are available. There
is also an ocean-view restaurant (see listing) and a gift shop.
Each beautifully furnished room has an honor bar. Oceanfront
rooms have a private balcony with bay/ocean view and some
others have a standing balcony.

★ **The Jabberwock** *(831)372-4777   (888)428-7253*
1 mi. NW at 598 Laine St. - 93940
jabberwockinn.com
8 units   *Expensive–Very Expensive*

A convent above Cannery Row has been charmingly transformed into a bed-and-breakfast inn with a museum-load of
quality antique furnishings and arts and crafts surrounded by
a luxuriant half acre of intimate gardens including a waterfall.
Amenities include a hearty breakfast and evening tea, cookies,
wine and appetizers. Each room is attractively individually
furnished. Several have a gas fireplace and whirlpool bath.

"Borogove"—spacious, gas fireplace, in-room two-person
whirlpool, windows on three sides, superb bay view.

"Mome Rath"—bayview windows, gas fireplace, in-room
two-person whirlpool.

Laurel Inn & Conference Center *(831)449-2474*
 19 mi. E at 801 W Laurel Dr. - Salinas 93906
 laurelinnmotel.com
 139 units *Moderate*
This two-story motel and facility for small conferences is well
worth the drive for budget-oriented travelers, especially on
weekends when rooms throughout the Peninsula are scarce and
dear. Amenities include a pool, whirlpool, sauna, and expanded
Continental breakfast, plus an on-premises chain restaurant.
Well-furnished rooms are nicely outfitted with plenty of lights
and have a refrigerator and microwave.

Lone Oak Motel *(831)372-4924* *(800)283-5663*
 2 mi. E at 2221 Fremont St. - 93940
 loneoaklodge.com
 46 units *Expensive*
Whirlpool, sauna and exercise equipment are features of
this single-level motel. Each compact contemporized room is
comfortably furnished including a refrigerator. Some have a
gas fireplace, a whirlpool in separate room, or a kitchen.

★ **Mariposa Inn & Suites** *(831)649-1414* *(800)824-2295*
 1 mi. S at 1386 Munras Av. - 93940
 mariposamonterey.com
 50 units *Moderate–Expensive*
This keystone lodging at the south end of Monterey's upscale
"motel row" is a contemporary two-story motel with a luxuriant
garden terrace and a large outdoor pool and whirlpool that
caters to romance. Expanded Continental breakfast is complimentary. Most beautifully furnished units have a raised gas

fireplace and/or in-room whirlpool, and all have a refrigerator and microwave. Four special rooms have both a raised gas log fireplace and an in-room two-person whirlpool.

★ **Monterey Bay Inn**   *(831)373-6242   (800)424-6242*
1 mi. NW at 242 Cannery Row - 93940
montereybayinn.com
49 units   Expensive–Very Expensive
Arguably Monterey's finest inn has a spectacular site by a sandy cove overlooking the National Marine Sanctuary on the bay at the quiet end of Cannery Row. The posh, post-modern four-story complex also features a rooftop with a spectacular ocean view and a courtyard whirlpool, plus a treatment room (good for couples). Expanded Continental breakfast served to the room is complimentary, as are cookies in the afternoon. Most of the beautifully furnished rooms have a refrigerator, a window wall and large private balcony with an ocean view. Waves lap against dramatic rock formations adjoining the enchanting rooms on the bay side.
    #411–#414—oceanfront view rooms, top floor, private
            super views of the bay.
    #220, #320—jetted two-person whirlpool tub with
            spectacular corner window bay and beach view.

★ **Monterey Bay Lodge**   *(831)372-8057*
just E at 55 Camino Aguajito - 93940
montereybaylodge.com
45 units   Moderate
Monterey's prettiest park is across the street from this fully remodeled single-level garden court motel. The coast and wharf are a short attractive stroll as well. A curvilinear pool is ensconced amid flower-strewn gardens backed by a giant magnolia and ancient Monterey Pines. The on-site **Bay Cafe** (B–L—Moderate) serves contemporary American fare and has attractive park-view windows. Each room is well furnished and includes a refrigerator and microwave. Several rooms also have a raised gas fireplace and a patio on the courtyard, and one has an in-room whirlpool.

The Monterey Hotel   *(831)375-3184   (800)966-6490*
downtown at 406 Alvarado St. - 93940

montereyhotel.com

69 units   *Moderate–Very Expensive*

The only small hotel in downtown Monterey is a four-story hotel (circa 1904) on the main street that has been skillfully restored. Expanded Continental breakfast and (in summer) afternoon refreshments are complimentary. Each room is attractively furnished including Victorian-style accents, and a refrigerator on request.

> "Fireplace Suite" (4 of these)—spacious, sitting area with gas fireplace, refrigerator/wet bar.

Monterey Marriott   *(831)649-4234*   *(888)236-2427*
downtown at 350 Calle Principal - 93940
marriott.com

341 units   *Expensive–Very Expensive*

Monterey's tallest landmark is a modern ten-story convention-oriented hotel in the heart of downtown and near the waterfront. Amenities include a pool, whirlpool, exercise room, (fee) parking, restaurant and sports bar. Well-furnished rooms have a refrigerator and (on request) microwave. The top three floors have appealing views of the marina and wharfs.

★ **Monterey Plaza Hotel & Spa**   *(831)920-6710*
1 mi. NW at 400 Cannery Row - 93940
montereyplazahotel.com

291 units   *Expensive–Very Expensive*

Monterey's most urbane full-service hotel is in an idyllic bayfront location on Cannery Row. Amenities of the handsome five-story complex include beach access, two whirlpools, sauna, steam room and exercise equipment, an elegant rooftop spa (**Vista Blue Spa**, see listing), **Helmsman** view lounge plus **Schooners**, a fine dining restaurant (see listing), and **Cafe La Strada** (B–L) for light fare. Each spacious room is beautifully furnished. Many have a large private balcony over the bay/ocean.

> #1302, #1202, #1102, #1002—corner, balcony over bay, floor-to-ceiling windows with superb water view.

Monterey Surf Inn   *(831)372-5821*
just S at 1200 Munras Av. - 93940
montereysurfinn.com

30 units   *Moderate*
After the latest remodel and upgrade, the Surf Motel is (by Monterey standards) usually a bargain. Conveniently located, amenities include a seasonal outdoor pool centered in the attractively landscaped one-story motel complex. Each comfortably outfitted unit includes a refrigerator and microwave.
Monterey Tides   *(831)394-3321*
2 mi. E at 2600 Sand Dunes Dr. - 93940
jdvhotels.com
196 units   *Expensive–Very Expensive*
Monterey Tides is the only major property in town directly on miles of sandy beach beyond the sheltered wharfs and marinas of Monterey Bay. The four-story hotel has undergone a complete makeover. It now offers a pool, whirlpool, exercise room, restaurant (**Cafe Beach**—B–L–D) with a panoramic Pacific Ocean view, and entertainment lounge. Many of the well-furnished rooms have a dramatic view of the beach and surf beyond a public access walkway in front of each unit.
   "Oceanside"—spectacular close-up view of ocean waves.
Munras Inn   *(831)646-9696*
just S at 1010 Munras Av. - 93940
munrasinn.com
29 units   *Moderate*
An easy stroll from downtown, Munras Inn is a contemporary motel which offers a sheltered courtyard with a whirlpool and sauna. Continental breakfast is complimentary. Each room is spacious, completely upgraded in 2016, and now well furnished including a microwave and refrigerator. Most have a raised gas fireplace. Several have an in-room two-person whirlpool and a gas fireplace.
★ **Old Monterey Inn**   *(831)375-8284*   *(800)350-2344*
just SW at 500 Martin St. - 93940
oldmontereyinn.com
10 units   *Very Expensive*
Old Monterey Inn is the most enchanting bed-and-breakfast in Monterey. A 1929 English Tudor-style mansion is sequestered amid luxuriant English gardens on a hillside. Bountiful gourmet breakfast and later, wine and cheese and fresh-baked cookies, are complimentary. Each spacious, romantically decorated

room is beautifully individually furnished with quality antiques and has a gas fireplace. Several units have additional notable features.

"Garden Cottage"—private cottage with in-room
　　two-person whirlpool with skylight.
"The Library"—large oak-view windows on
　　three sides, private oak-shaded deck.
"Mayfield Suite"—romantic, wisteria view,
　　two-person in-room whirlpool.
"Chawton"—private entrance through gardens,
　　marble two-person whirlpool.

Portola Hotel & Spa　*(831)649-4511*　*(888)222-5851*
downtown at 2 Portola Plaza - 93940
portolahotel.com
379 units　　　　　　　　　*Expensive–Very Expensive*
This modern hotel is a seven-story convention-and-conference-oriented landmark occupying a choice location between downtown and Fisherman's Wharf. Amenities in addition to close proximity to the bay include a pool, whirlpool, full-service body/beauty spa, fitness center, restaurant (see listing), lounge, and micro-brew pub. Some of the well-furnished rooms have a private balcony. Some have a nearby bay view from the top three floors.

7th (top) floor (7 of these) "executive king"—
　　panoramic bay/town views,
　　(only #702 has a balcony).
5th and 6th floors—fine harbor/bay view.

Sanctuary Beach Resort　*(831)88309478*　*(877)944-3863*
8 mi. NE (via Hwy. 1) at 3295 Dunes Dr. - Marina 93933
thesanctuarybeachresort.com
60 units　　　　　　　　　　　　*Very Expensive*
One of the area's newest bayfront lodgings shares a remote sandy beach and (view-only) windswept dunes at the far eastern end of Monterey Bay with an upscale time-share complex. Guests have restricted beach path access (but you cannot walk on the dunes), a pool and whirlpool, spa services, and an on-site restaurant. All spacious, beautifully furnished units have a gas fireplace, refrigerator, microwave, and private deck with a bay or dunes view.

★ **Spindrift Inn**   *(831)646-8900*
   1 mi. NW at 652 Cannery Row - 93940
   spindriftinn.com
   45 units   *Expensive–Very Expensive*
Spindrift Inn is one of California's most romantic lodgings. The gracious contemporary getaway is above a narrow picturesque beach in the midst of Cannery Row. Continental breakfast is served when you schedule it to your room, and afternoon wine and cheese are complimentary. Each individually decorated, beautifully furnished room has a fireplace (all but three are wood-burning), and a window seat or private deck. Many have an unforgettable close-up bayfront view. For a rare, truly memorable experience, get a waterfront room on a really stormy day, when the normally calm bayside waters are whipped into full Pacific Ocean waves and breathtaking surf explodes against solid rocks and reinforced foundation of the inn.
   #407, #307, #207 (corner king deluxe rooms)—grand
         bay view, wood-burning fireplace, window seats.
Villa Franca Inn   *(831)373-2921   (800)722-1836*
   just S at 900 Munras Av. - 93940
   villafrancainn.com
   15 units   *Expensive*
Downtown is an easy stroll from this convenient, contemporary little motel. Continental breakfast is complimentary. Each room was attractively remodeled and upgraded in 2016 and has a refrigerator and microwave. Four units have a wood-burning fireplace; and Room 14 also has some distant bay view.

BASIC INFORMATION

Elevation: 40 feet   Population (2010):   27,810
Location: 120 miles South of San Francisco
Nearest airport with commercial flights: in town
Monterey County Convention & Visitors Bureau
   downtown at 787 Munras Ave. #10 - 93940
   seemonterey.com   (800)555-6290
Monterey Visitors Information Center   (888)221-1010
   just E at 401 Camino El Estero
Monterey Peninsula Chamber of Commerce   (831)648-5360
   downtown at 243 El Dorado St. #200 - 93940
   montereychamber.com   73

Pacific Grove, California

HISTORY & DESCRIPTION

Pacific Grove is a seaside haven of tranquility. Situated along a strikingly beautiful coastline where the waters of the Pacific Ocean and Monterey Bay converge, the town is favored by a mild year-round climate. Methodists, drawn by the peaceful setting and the idyllic climate, founded the town in 1875 as a summer retreat. Strict ordinances on personal behavior (drinking, dancing, profanity, and even swimming) lasted for nearly a century. In fact it wasn't until 1969 that residents voted to permit the sale of alcohol in what had been California's last "dry" town. The legacy of the austere early settlers was the creation of a genteel haven amidst extravagant surroundings.

Today, Pacific Grove continues to evolve as a refined refuge. Lovingly maintained and upgraded Victorian homes and shops predominate amid landscapes of mature trees and luxuriant gardens. Shoreline parks, sandy beaches, coves and miles of winding paths frame the Pacific Ocean and Monterey Bay perimeters of town. Inland, trim Victorian houses amid colorful floral displays and carefully tended lawns line serene tree-shaded streets. The tidy feeling of a nineteenth-century New England village has been meticulously retained, especially downtown. Sophisticated galleries, shops, and gourmet restaurants are features of the classic district. Accommodations range from some of the nation's finest Victorian-era bed-and-breakfast inns to comfortable motels. Several lodgings are clustered near a shady forest that is the famed winter home of vast numbers of monarch butterflies. The annual concentration inevitably resulted in the town's nickname, "Butterfly Town, U.S.A."

WEATHER

Pacific Grove occupies the picturesque northwestern tip of the Monterey Peninsula. Most of the town is sheltered from direct exposure to Pacific Ocean breezes by sand dunes and gentle hills covered with Monterey Pines and mature trees. It shares (with Monterey and Carmel) one of America's most desirable climates for comfortably enjoying outdoor recreation. Mild conditions prevail year-round, except in winter where cool frost-free weather is the norm, but rainstorms contribute more than half of the average annual precipitation. In spring, warm mild days begin, showers diminish, and fog and sea breezes become more common. Two fascinating natural phenomena occur in their respective seasons. Vast numbers of Monarch butterflies return to their favorite trees on the west side of town for the winter; and the slopes along the bayfront parks salute spring as dense carpets of tiny iceplants become flamboyant masses of vivid pinkish flowers. Summer's warm, rainless days (occasionally marred by fog) are perfect for enjoying seaside adventures. Fall normally brings the year's highest temperatures. Ideal conditions prevail until after Thanksgiving, when the rainy season begins again in earnest.

WEATHER PROFILE

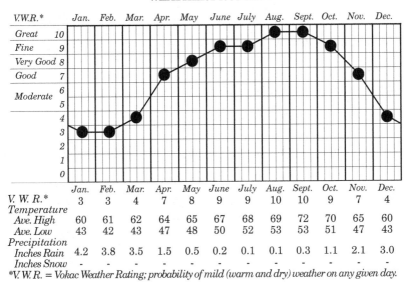

V.W.R.*	Jan.	Feb.	Mar.	Apr.	May	June	July	Aug.	Sept.	Oct.	Nov.	Dec.
V. W. R.*	3	3	4	7	8	9	9	10	10	9	7	4
Temperature												
Ave. High	60	61	62	64	65	67	68	69	72	70	65	60
Ave. Low	43	42	43	47	48	50	52	53	53	51	47	43
Precipitation												
Inches Rain	4.2	3.8	3.5	1.5	0.5	0.2	0.1	0.1	0.3	1.1	2.1	3.0
Inches Snow	-	-	-	-	-	-	-	-	-	-	-	-

*V. W. R. = Vokac Weather Rating; probability of mild (warm and dry) weather on any given day.

ATTRACTIONS

★ *Bicycling*
The Monterey Peninsula Recreation Trail follows one of the
most scenic stretches of coastline in California for almost
twenty miles from Asilomar in Pacific Grove to Castroville. The
separated bikeway accommodates both bicyclists and pedaled
surreys as it meanders past colorful parks and popular beaches
along Pacific Grove's entire shoreline. Another renowned bike
route is the incomparable Seventeen-Mile Drive (there is a fee
for auto drivers, but none for bicyclists) which extends from
the edge of Pacific Grove to the southern side of the Peninsula
at Carmel.
 Adventures by the Sea *(831)372-1807*
 downtown at the beach at Lovers Point
 adventuresbythesea.com
Golf
★ **Pacific Grove Golf Links** *(831)648-5775*
 1 mi. NW via Lighthouse Av. at 77 Asilomar Coastal Trail
 playpacificgrove.com
On this historic, 18-hole municipal course, the entire back nine
features splendid ocean-view fairways among low dunes and
woodlands. In addition, this is the Peninsula's most affordable
golf experience near the Pacific Ocean. There is a full-service
golf shop, driving range, and clubhouse with **Point Pinos
Grill** (B–L–D) providing panoramic views of the bay and a
good assortment of California fare for all meals.
★ **Lovers Point** *(831)648-5730*
 just N at the bay end of 17th St./Oceanview Blvd.
A small bayside park combines sandy coves, dramatic rock
formations, Monterey cypress, and green lawns into one of
the Peninsula's most romantic and photogenic highlights. The
ocean here is normally clear and relatively safe, apart from
winter storm surf which can be dramatic and dangerous. The
water off Bathhouse Beach is a favorite of hearty swimmers
in summer, and surfers (in wet suits) year-round. **The Grill**
(L–D—Moderate) offers salmon burgers, milkshakes and other
casual food to enjoy on a scenic picnic table by the beach.

★ **The Magic Carpet of "Mesembryanthemum"**
just N along the bay
This fanciful tongue-twister is the name for masses of succulent ice plants that drape a long stretch of Monterey Bay shoreline northwest of Lovers Point. From April through August, a solid lavender-pink carpet of tiny flowers covers the iceplants with a brilliant mantle above the rockbound bay.

★ **Monarch Grove Sanctuary** *(831)648-5716*
1 mi. W at 250 Ridge Rd. just S of Lighthouse Av.
cityofpacificgrove.org/visiting/monarch-butterfly-sanctuary
Pacific Grove is known as "Butterfly Town, U.S.A." This is because one of the town's major attractions is the Monarch Butterfly which, from November through March, becomes a resident of the grove of trees here near the tip of the peninsula for over-wintering. Native flowering plants provide nourishment and towering Eucalyptus trees provide shelter. When they are in residence in massive numbers, portions of the trees seem to actually turn from green to bright orange. The best viewing is late morning to early afternoon when the sun warms their wings and during mating season in January and February. Follow the marked path into the forest where volunteer docents are usually available from noon to 3 p.m. in winter with a telescope and helpful information.

★ **Pacific Grove Museum of Natural History** *(831)648-5716*
downtown at 165 Forest Av.
pgmuseum.org
Pacific Grove's well-regarded museum (circa 1883) is one of America's first natural history museums. It has a notable exhibit dealing with the phenomenon of the Monarch butterfly trees. Also, a large relief map of the Peninsula and bay graphically depicts the great chasm of Monterey Bay which plummets within a few miles from shore deeper than the Grand Canyon. Near the entrance is a life-sized model of a female grey whale.

Point Pinos Lighthouse
1 mi. W at west end of Lighthouse Av. at 80 Asilomar Av.
pointpinoslighthouse.org
The oldest continuously operating lighthouse on the Pacific Coast has stood at the entrance to Monterey Bay since 1855. It

sits in the center of a golf course now, and is open to the public on Thursday through Sunday between 1 and 4 p.m.

★ **Seventeen-Mile Drive** *(866)990-6895*
starts just W via Lighthouse Av. to Seventeen-Mile Dr.
pebblebeach.com
One of the world's great scenic roadways meanders past spectacularly landscaped estates in Pebble Beach and along the splendid coastline between Pacific Grove and Carmel. It is paved, and a toll road except to residents and bicyclists. However, the gate fee is reimbursed with a purchase of $30 or more in resort restaurants (hold onto your entry receipt). Gnarled trees clinging to rocky headlands at **The Lone Cypress** are among the West's most photographed landmarks.

★ **Shoreline Parks** *(831)648-5730*
N & W on Ocean View Blvd. & Sunset Dr.
cityofpacificgrove.org/visiting
A continuous series of seaside parks along Monterey Bay provide access to numerous tiny sandy beaches tucked into coves along rocky headlands. On the ocean side beyond **Point Pinos Lighthouse** (the oldest—1855—continuously operating lighthouse on the Pacific Coast), the rocky shoreline drive is flanked for nearly a mile by low grassy sand dunes and pines in photogenic **Asilomar State Beach**. Sunset Drive turns inland near Pacific Grove's southern city limit.

RESTAURANTS

Aliotti's Victorian Corner   *(831)372-4641*
downtown at 541 Lighthouse Av.
victoriancornerpg.com
B–L–D.   *Moderate*
For nearly forty years, Pacific Grove's classiest little Victorian building has been a family-owned favorite. Today, traditional and updated American specialties include crab benedicts, almond pancakes, walnut waffles, and San Francisco Joe omelets. Wood-trim tables and chairs are surrounded by nostalgic pictures and high-ceilinged window views of downtown.

★ **Beach House at Lovers Point**   *(831)375-2345*
just N at 620 Ocean View Blvd. at Lovers Point Beach
beachhousepg.com
D only.   *Moderate*
Pacific Grove's landmark dinner house has a winning way with creative American cuisine that changes seasonally, like salmon and corn chowder, Portobello fries, or hazelnut-crusted sand dabs, and housemade luscious desserts like mud pie. But it is the enchanting view of Monterey Bay and Lovers Point beyond a little sandy cove beach, complemented by casually comfortable decor in an ingeniously converted Victorian bathhouse, that assures continuing status as one of California's most romantic restaurants. Because the picture windows frame the delightful view to the east, staff doesn't have to close the shades while the sun sets.

★ **Bookworks Coffee House**   *(831)372-2242*
downtown at 667 Lighthouse Av.
B–L.   *Moderate*
Pacific Grove's most appealing coffee house captures the spirit of the town in a shaped-up serene shop with a choice of tables and chairs or sofa seating. A display case shows off a tempting variety of morning delights like lemon tea cake and apple walnut coffee cake made by the owner, plus pastries, muffins, scones, etc. from key local sources. The coffee house extends into Pacific Grove's bookstore where readers can still enjoy turning pages of a good selection of regional and national titles.

Crema Espresso & Wine Bar   *(831)324-0347*
downtown at 481 Lighthouse Av.
cremapg.com
B–L.   *Moderate*
They serve breakfast (except Sun.-Mon.) but come for the
housemade baked goods downstairs. Half a dozen kinds of
morning delights (including a stellar bacon-and-cheese biscuit)
are displayed to go with assorted coffees or enjoy them in one
of several little dining areas of a transformed Victorian home.

★ **Fandango**   *(831)372-3456*
downtown at 223 17th St.
fandangorestaurant.com
L–D. Sun. brunch.   *Expensive*
Fandango, opened more than thirty years ago, offers Pacific
Grove's longest-established fine dining experience. Authentic
and innovative European country-style cuisine includes dishes
from an open mesquite grill like big Black Angus Porterhouse
steaks or double lamb chops. Paella and sautéed sand dabs are
other flavorful specialties. Save room for housemade desserts
like Grand Marnier soufflé or lemon cheesecake. Full linen
and fresh flowers enliven a series of colorful, romantic little
dining rooms, a firelit conservatory, and full bar.

Fifi's Cafe   *(831)372-5325*
1 mi. S at 1188 Forest Av.
fifiscafe.com
L–D. L only on Fri. Sun. brunch.   *Moderate*
A small corner shop in a shopping center has been artfully
transformed into a bistro where the French owner offers a
well-thought-out menu ranging from escargot or steamed
mussels to filet mignon. A comfortable congestion of tables
outfitted with linen and flowers is surrounded by racks of wine
for sale and colorful Gallic touches.

First Awakenings   *(831)372-1125*
1 mi. E at 125 Oceanview Blvd. (in American Tin Cannery)
firstawakenings.net
B–L.   *Moderate*
Pancakes, assorted omelets, crepes, and thick French toast are
morning highlights. This bright, plant-filled coffee shop with
an adjoining dining deck has been popular for years.

Fishwife at Asilomar Beach   *(831)375-7107*
1 mi. SW at 1996½ Sunset Dr. at Asilomar Beach
fishwife.com
L–D.   *Moderate*
Fresh seasonal fish include some real hits given a light,
bright touch on a contemporary California menu with Italian,
Mexican and Cajun influences. Desserts like key lime pie
are homemade. Casual little dining areas surround a wood-
trimmed bar in the original location of the fish house with
an outpost in Seaside.

★ **Il Vecchio**   *(831)324-4282*
1 mi. E at 110 Central Av.
ilvecchiorestaurant.com
L–D. No L Sat. & Sun.   *Moderate*
Roman and Tuscan dishes ranging from mussels or shrimp to
wild rock cod or ribeye steak get support from classic Italian
antipasti, soups and salads, plus housemade pasta and pizza
made fresh every day. A historic building now sports an
easygoing trattoria look appropriate for enjoying authentic
Italian cuisine.

★ **La Mia Cucina**   *(831)373-2416*
downtown at 208 17th St.
lamiacucinaristorante.com
D only. Closed Mon.–Tues.   *Moderate*
In this family-owned-and-operated young culinary landmark,
classic Italian cuisine and some inspired flourishes are
skillfully executed for a thoughtful selection of dishes. Consider
spinach salad with a fine vinaigrette, nuts, cheese, and as
a delightful enhancement, dried cherries. Entrees might
include a delectable lobster ravioli with cream sauce, or petrale
sole Doré. All are served with fine homemade focaccia to be
dipped in vinegar and oil. Equally distinguished desserts
include historic family specialties like sherry pound cake
drizzled with secret sauce coupled with homemade pistachio
ice cream. The inviting, intimate dining room benefits from
full linen, crystal and candles backed by colorful poster art
as an appropriate setting for some of the Peninsula's most
exciting gourmet cuisine.

Passionfish   *(831)655-3311*
downtown at 701 Lighthouse Av.
passionfish.net
D only.   *Moderate*
A selection of seafood (based on sustainability rather than freshness or locally caught) is featured on a creative, ever-changing menu. Examples might include Dungeness crabcake with avocado salad or trout with basil, as well as unusual desserts served in simply outfitted dining rooms.

★ **Patisserie Bechler**   *(831)375-0846*
1 mi. S at 1225 Forest Av.
patisseriebechler.com
B–L. Closed Mon. No L Sun.   *Moderate*
Competition for the finest bakery on the Monterey Peninsula really starts with Bechler. A splendid large display of triple-racked morning delights in the front room ranges from classic Continental specialties like croissants (in both large and small sizes) to creative contemporary adaptations like blueberry-almond tart. A wealth of exquisite cakes displays the skill and artistry of the owner/chef. Lunch is similarly popular in assorted sandwiches on a croissant, french or wheat roll; plus specialties like crepes, spinach wrap or chicken quesadillas that can be accompanied by soup or salad. Hardwood round tables and comfortable armchairs distinguish an expansive skylit dining room with a window wall on three sides.

★ **Pavel's Bäckerei**   *(831)643-2636*
downtown at 219 Forest Av.
B–L. Closed Sun.–Mon.   *Moderate*
Pavel's is another of the best bakeries on the Peninsula. Delicious bear claws, danishes, cinnamon rolls, and bagels are backed by unusual treats like francesse (white flour pillow), white cheddar cheese bagels and nine-grain rolls and loaves, plus designer cakes. When they are available, don't miss their unique "scoffin" (a blend of a scone and a muffin) which captures the best of both. Their lunch sandwiches are also first rate. There are a few tables for enjoying morning delights here with coffee, but most customers grab and go with their delights.

★ **Peppers Mexicali Cafe**   *(831)373-6892*
downtown at 170 Forest Av.
peppersmexicalicafe.com
L–D. No L Sun. Closed Tues.   *Moderate*
Excellent innovations like curry prawns with mango salsa
or grilled snapper with chiles, citrus and cilantro are among
Mexican/American dishes served in the cozy congestion of a
wood-trimmed dining room and bar. Consistently first-rate
dishes have made this competition for the most deservedly
popular Mexican specialty restaurant on the Peninsula.

Red House Cafe   *(831)643-1060*
downtown at 662 Lighthouse Av.
redhousecafe.com
B–L–D. No D on Mon.   *Moderate*
One of the Peninsula's longest-established independent restaurants is still a favorite with locals and travelers for breakfast.
American comfort dishes like large pancakes with a choice
of bananas or berries in the batter are consistently carefully
prepared. Meals can be enjoyed in a Victorian cottage with
a firelit entry room amid a cozy congestion of rooms or on a
porch with a close-up view of downtown.

Taste Cafe & Bistro   *(831)655-0324*
1 mi. S at 1199 Forest Av.
tastecafebistro.com
D only. Closed Mon.   *Expensive*
The chef/owner's traditional and creative fare is given careful
attention in dishes like salmon fillet baked in parchment paper.
Toothsome desserts made here also contribute to the appeal of
simply stylish dining rooms with fanciful wall and ceiling art.

LODGINGS

Accommodations are numerous. Most are small and independent, including several delightful bed-and-breakfast inns. Summer and fall are prime time. Rates are often reduced 20% or more (apart from weekends) in winter.

★ **Andril Fireplace Cottages**   *(831)375-0994*
1 mi. W at 569 Asilomar Blvd. - 93950
andrilcottages.com
24 units   *Moderate–Expensive*
Tucked into a pine forest, Andril provides choices from a standard motel-style room all the way to a cottage with a full kitchen, wood-burning fireplace, and whirlpool tub. Amenities include ping pong, and scenic paths and byways an easy stroll to nearby Pacific Ocean beaches. Each well-furnished unit has a private patio and refrigerator.
   Luxury Cottage (4 of these)—wood-burning
      fireplace, whirlpool, full kitchen.

Best Western Inn & Suites - Pacific Grove   *(831)373-8777*
1 mi. W at 660 Dennett St. - 93950   (800)528-1234
montereypgbw.com
30 units   *Very Expensive*
These tucked-away converted condo/townhouses are spacious and well-furnished. Many include a full kitchen.

Borg's Ocean Front Motel   *(831)375-2406*
just N at 635 Ocean View Blvd. - 93950
borgsoceanfrontmotel.com
60 units   *Moderate*
Some of Borg's rooms have views across a street to Lovers Point bayfront park. Each room in the long-established two-story motel is simply furnished. Many have a picture-window view of the ocean just beyond a picturesque rocky coastline.
   #150—spacious, bayview windows on two sides.

★ **Butterfly Grove Inn**   *(831)250-8191*
1 mi. W at 1073 Lighthouse Av. - 93950
butterflygroveinn.com
30 units   *Moderate*
This well-maintained largely-single-level motel on subtropically landscaped grounds is immediately adjacent to the spectacular **Monarch Grove Sanctuary** (see listing) which is accessible

by an adjoining walkway. Other amenities include a large heated pool and an oversized whirlpool. Continental breakfast is complimentary. Each spacious, well-furnished room has been recently remodeled and now includes a refrigerator and microwave. Some have a whirlpool bath or kitchenette.

#26A, 26B—in back, upstairs, windows
directly overlook butterfly trees.

★ **Centrella Bed & Breakfast Inn**   *(831)372-3372*
   downtown at 612 Central Av. - 93950   (800)233-3372
   centrellainn.com
   25 units   *Expensive*
A Victorian building (circa 1889) an easy stroll from ocean parks is now a large, well-landscaped bed-and-breakfast inn. Full hot breakfast, evening glass of wine and appetizers, and homemade chocolate chip cookies are complimentary. Each well-furnished room, suite and cottage combines old-time antiques with new furnishings. Cottages also have a gas fireplace.

"Garden Room Suite"—pot-belly gas stove, two-
person whirlpool tub, wet bar, canopy bed.

★ **Gosby House - A Four Sisters Inn**   *(831)375-1287*
   downtown at 643 Lighthouse Av. - 93950   (800)527-8828
   gosbyhouseinn.com
   22 units   *Moderate–Expensive*
The ocean is a convenient stroll from this authentic Victorian mansion amid carefully tended gardens in the heart of town. It now serves as a tastefully furnished bed-and-breakfast inn with nostalgic charm. A full buffet breakfast is included, as are afternoon appetizers and wine, plus cookies. All rooms are individually attractively furnished including some antiques.

"Superior King Spa" (3 of these)—two-person in-bath
whirlpool, gas fireplace, private balcony.

★ **Green Gables - A Four Sisters Inn**   *(831)375-2095*
   just E at 301 Ocean View Blvd. - 93950   (800)722-1774
   greengablesinnpg.com   (800)722-1774
   11 units   *Moderate–Expensive*
One of California's most beguiling Queen Anne-style mansions (circa 1888) has been meticulously transformed into a romantic bed-and-breakfast inn. The photogenic main house and carriage house are on lovely grounds across a street from the bay.

Spectacular rock outcroppings and surf views distinguish the world-class backdrop. Full breakfast and afternoon wine and appetizers are complimentary. Use of bicycles is also complimentary to enjoy the coastal bike/hike path across the street. While rooms vary in size, and some share bathrooms, all are beautifully furnished, including fine period pieces and decor. Some have a gas fireplace and/or a romantic bay/ocean view.

"Carriage House Rooms" (4 of these)—
        sitting area, some ocean views,
        in-bath two-person whirlpool
        tub, gas fireplace.
"Lacy Suite"—spacious parlor with some
        bay view, gas fireplace,
        in-bath whirlpool.
"Jennifer"—in-bath whirlpool, window seat
        with some bay view.

Lighthouse Lodge & Cottages *(831)655-2111*
1 mi. W at 1150 Lighthouse Av. - 93950
lighthouselodgecottages.com
95 units   *Moderate–Very Expensive*
The ocean is a stroll from this contemporary wood-shingled quiet and quaint cottage complex amid pines and gardens. Guests have access to a pool and whirlpool in the **Lodge** (a 64-unit motel) across the street. Full breakfast and evening wine and appetizers are complimentary to **Cottage** guests. Continental breakfast is complimentary to Lodge guests. The well-furnished Cottage suites have a gas fireplace and a large whirlpool bath. All units have both a refrigerator and microwave.

Lovers Point Inn *(831)373-4771   (866)785-0355*
just N at 625 Ocean View Blvd. - 93950
loverspointinnpg.com
50 units   *Moderate*
Lovers Point Park and beach are across the street from this older motel with a complimentary Continental breakfast. Each simply furnished room has a refrigerator and microwave. Third floor rooms have some ocean views.

★ **Martine Inn**   *(831)373-3388   (800)852-5588*
   just E at 255 Ocean View Blvd. - 93950
   martineinn.com
   23 units   *Expensive–Very Expensive*
A large Mediterranean-style villa built in the late 1890s on a rise
across a street from the bay is now a luxurious bed-and-breakfast inn surrounded by colorful gardens. Full museum-quality
silver-service breakfast, afternoon appetizers and refreshments
including red and white wine are complimentary, as is use of
the game room billiard and ping pong tables. Premium-quality
period pieces used throughout contribute to the genteel appeal
of this romantic retreat. Each room is beautifully furnished.
Most have a clawfoot tub and bay/ocean view. Two also have
a wood-burning fireplace.
   "The Suite"—corner windows with grand bay view,
         corner wood-burning fireplace, porcelain tub.
   "Parke"—bayview windows on 3 sides, corner wood-
         burning fireplace, clawfoot tub, bay view from
         four-poster canopy bed.
   "Eastlake"—windows provide fine bay view from both
         seven-foot clawfoot tub and raised canopy bed.

Monarch Resort   *(831)646-8885*
   1 mi. W at 1111 Lighthouse Av. - 93950
   monarchresortmontereybay.com
   50 units   *Moderate*
Amenities of this recently refurbished motel include an outdoor
pool, whirlpool, and sauna. Continental breakfast is complimentary. Each comfortably furnished room has a refrigerator. Most
have a private balcony. Several also have a wood-burning fireplace.

Old St. Angela Inn   *(831)372-3246*
   just E at 321 Central Av. - 93950
   oldstangelainn.com
   9 units   *Moderate–Expensive*
A historic Craftsman-style mansion one block from the hike/
bike path along Monterey Bay has evolved into a bed-and-
breakfast with a whirlpool in a garden. A full hot breakfast and
afternoon wine and cookies are complimentary. All rooms are
compact, and individually well furnished including nostalgic
touches. Some have a gas fireplace and/or a whirlpool tub.

★ **Pacific Gardens Inn** *(831)646-9414*
  1 mi. W at 701 Asilomar Blvd. - 93950
  pacificgardensinn.com
  28 units   *Moderate*
This recently remodeled/upgraded motel in the pines is a
short walk from an ocean beach. There are two whirlpools.
Continental breakfast from a local bakery and wine and cheese
in the afternoon are complimentary. Each well-furnished room
includes a refrigerator. Most have a wood-burning fireplace.

★ **Rosedale Inn** *(831)655-1000 (800)822-5606*
  1 mi. W at 775 Asilomar Blvd. - 93950
  rosedaleinn.com
  19 units   *Moderate–Expensive*
This quiet, well-regarded complex was recently upgraded.
Asilomar Conference Center is across a street and there are
trails leading through the surrounding woods to a nearby ocean
beach. Expanded Continental breakfast is complimentary. Each
room is well furnished including a whirlpool tub, gas fireplace,
refrigerator and microwave.

★ **Seven Gables Inn** *(831)372-4341*
  just N at 555 Ocean View Blvd. - 93950
  thesevengablesinn.com
  27 units   *Very Expensive*
Seven Gables Inn reigns as one of California's most outstanding
bed-and-breakfasts. Monterey Bay and Lovers Point are across
the street from an exquisitely restored expansive complex
surrounded by colorful gardens that includes a Victorian
mansion, beach house, and related nostalgic cottages. Full
breakfast amid classic elegance, and afternoon wine and
cheese and cookies, are complimentary. As an added adult
treat, selected local wineries visit and pour Wednesday through
Saturday. Each beautifully furnished room has a wealth of
authentic European antiques. Many have a bay (ocean) view.
  "Cypress Room"—romantic, spacious, refrigerator,
        corner, window with grand panoramic bay view.
  "Ocean Mist"—spacious, refrigerator,
        grand panoramic bay view.
  "Breakers"—corner room with many fine bay-
        view windows, refrigerator, gas fireplace.

Sunset Inn   *(831)375-3529   (866)550-7550*
1 mi. W at 133 Asilomar Blvd. - 93950
gosunsetinn.com
22 units   *Moderate*
In a quiet pine forest and deer haven an easy stroll from
the ocean is a recently remodeled inn with a complimentary
Continental breakfast. Each attractively furnished room is
individually decorated and has a refrigerator. Four rooms have
both a gas fireplace and in-bath two-person whirlpool. One
room has a full kitchen and expansive view.

BASIC INFORMATION

Elevation: 50 feet   Population (2010):   15,081
Location: 125 miles South of San Francisco
Nearest airport with commercial flights: Monterey - 4 miles
Pacific Grove Chamber of Commerce
    Downtown Tourist Information Center   (831)373-3304
        584 Central Av. - 93950
        Open Mon.–Fri. 9:30–5
        pacificgrove.org
    Pacific Grove Tourist Information Center   (831)324-4668
        100 Central Av., near Monterey Bay Aquarium
        Open daily 10–5

End Notes

This book uses the same format and conventions from our comprehensive national guidebook, **The Great Towns of America**. For the convenience of anyone not familiar with that book, here is an explanation of the meaning of the book's major elements.

Weather Profile: the "Vokac Weather Rating"
The "Vokac Weather Rating" © (VWR) is a unique feature of all "Great Towns" guidebooks. It measures and graphically summarizes the probability of "pleasant weather" (warm, dry conditions suitable for outdoor recreation in light sportswear) for each month. Average high and low temperatures, rainfall, and snowfall are also provided. A proprietary algorithm is used to rate weather from "0" (intense weather requiring related suitable clothing) to "10" (ideal). Every increment of one on the VWR scale represents a 10% greater chance of pleasant weather. Generally, ratings of "7" or above indicate a high probability of desirable conditions for outdoor activity.

Locations, Ratings, Prices
Carmel, Monterey and Pacific Grove have very well-defined walkable downtowns and all mileage and directions (N, S, E or W for North, South, East or West) are calculated from a central point in each heart of town. In terms of ratings, every effort was made to include all of the places that we believe best convey the charm of the Peninsula. Key resorts, bed-and-breakfasts, hotels, and the best inexpensive motels in each area are featured. Comparable information is provided about the relative quality and cost of every lodging and restaurant. A star indicates the authors' favorites, and desirability is also reflected in each review's length.

Restaurants
The basic price information reflects the cost of an average dinner (soup or salad and entree) not including tip, tax, or beverage. Price categories are: Low: under $15; Moderate: $15–$30; Expensive: $30–$45; and Very Expensive: $45+. Meals that are served are indicated as B (breakfast), L (lunch) and D (dinner).

End Notes

Lodgings

In our other guidebooks we always used weekend rates to identify likely highest cost of a room. For this book, we used "weekday" rates because the Peninsula is unusual among great towns—rates are raised so signficantly on summer weekends that scarcely any rooms are offered for less than $100. Many properties also require a two- or three-night stay. Budget-minded travelers can ideally plan their visits for weekdays, or drive in from nearby Salinas for a substantial cost saving.

As a result, computations of costs were for high season (summer) *weekday* rack rates for a room sized for two people apart from discounts, special event variations, and local taxes. The categories for nightly costs are: Low: under $100; Moderate: $100–200; Expensive: $200–$300; and Very Expensive: over $300. When a range is shown for the price (e.g., Expensive–Very Expensive), it means that different types of rooms are available with room prices in those respective categories.

Some Final Comments

This guidebook is unusual in these ways:
(1) We personally visited all features, and have distilled them to include all of our determinations of the very best.
(2) No business paid to be included in this book, and no advertising was allowed.
(3) Websites for businesses are always included when available.
(4) All material is consistently arranged in a simple, uniform layout for ease of use.
(5) The quality of weather is rated for each month on a zero-to-ten scale using the copyrighted © Vokac Weather Rating.

All information has been carefully checked, and is believed to be current and accurate in 2016. No malice is intended or implied by the judgments expressed, nor by the omission of any facility or service from this book.

About the Authors

David Vokac has been dubbed the Guru of Great Towns. Since 1985 he has crisscrossed America again and again searching for ideal towns combining scenic grandeur, exhilarating outdoor recreation options, and strong regional culture. He believes that in small town America, the true diversity of this nation's geography and culture is captured best. Landscapes endowed with majestic mountains, raging rivers, lovely lakes and awe-inspiring oceans provide unique settings where people convene to play and relax. In these idyllic towns, visitors opt for outdoor activities like swimming, boating, hiking, or fishing, and enjoyment of manmade attractions like museums, parks, monuments, and specialty shops. Chefs get inspired with fresh regional ingredients and culinary traditions to create exciting dishes which celebrate local tastes. Visitors opt for lodgings ranging from convenient bargains or creative architectural expressions (like transformed mansions) to unique features ranging from rooms in treehouses to new age bubble-jet tubs.

David was inspired to focus his books on Great Towns by his youth in Cody, Wyoming where he rode horses, ran rivers, and fished in Yellowstone Lake while enjoying a first-rate education in a top-notch school system in the town founded by Buffalo Bill. His subsequent education including a Master of Arts in geography and area development led to professional work in community and park development which honed his interests and skills at finding desirable locales. Following two complete editions of the landmark guidebook about the 100 Great Towns of America, David continues to return to these favored venues and seek more of them to keep travelers updated on getaways and boondock features in this great country of ours, the United States of America.

Joan Vokac, after serving 35 years as a land use planner for the unincorporated villages of San Diego County, now joins husband David in seeking the most exciting getaway towns in the nation. She delights in discovering new towns combining physical grandeur with distinctive local culture. Whether spending a day gliding down a waterslide or hiking a trail, she enjoys returning to a gourmet meal and friendly lodging in one of America's Great Towns. In addition to being an avid researcher and co-author of the most recent Great Towns guidebooks, she is webmaster of greattowns.com and has become an occasional trainer due to her expertise gained from converting the Great Towns information into contemporary media.

To keep apprised of the Vokacs' travels, to add comments and suggestions regarding their work, for continuing updates on America's top getaways, and to find out about upcoming titles, visit *greattowns.com* and *facebook.com/greattowns*.

Index

A

B

Index

D

E

F

G

I

J

K

L

Index

Lodge at Pebble Beach
  Golf 13–14
  Horseback Riding 14
  Lodging 39–40
  Restaurants 29–30
  Spa 16
Lodgings
  Carmel 33–43
  Monterey 64–73
  Pacific Grove 84–89
Lone Cypress 78
Lone Oak Motel 68
Loulou's Griddle in the Middle 59
Lovers Point 76
Lovers Point Inn 86
Lucia Restaurant & Lounge 22

M

Magic Carpet of "Mesembryanthemum" 77
Manzoni 18
Marina 49
Marina State Beach 49
Mariposa Inn & Suites 68–69
Marriott 70
Martine Inn 87
Massaro & Santos 59
Mission Basilica 13
Mission Ranch
  Lodging 40
  Restaurant 30
Molera Big Sur Horseback Riding 8
Monarch Grove Sanctuary 77, 84–85
Monarch Resort 87
Monterey
  Attractions 46–53
  History 44
  Lodgings 64–73
  Restaurants 54–63
  Weather 45

Index

Index

Index

Travel Guidebooks by David & Joan Vokac

The most notable attractions, restaurants, and lodgings are described and rated for each of the nation's most exciting locales:

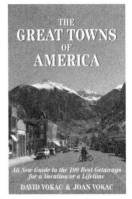

The Great Towns of America

*Guide to the 100 Best Getaways
for a Vacation or a Lifetime*

Print book $23.95
Second Edition 2009

Expansions and updates cover selected great towns with 45-page quality paperback guides covering all the best attractions, restaurants, lodgings, weather charts, and more.

These are also available in all electronic formats for $2.99 apiece.

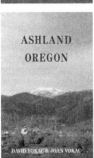

CPSIA information can be obtained
at www.ICGtesting.com
Printed in the USA
FSOW03n1425170616
21702FS